CISTERCIAN STUDIES SERIES: NUMBER ONE HUNDRED SEVENTY-SIX

Jean-Baptiste Van Damme, ocso

THE THREE FOUNDERS OF CÎTEAUX

CISTERCIAN STUDIES SERIES: NUMBER ONE HUNDRED SEVENTY-SIX

THE THREE FOUNDERS OF CÎTEAUX

Robert of Molesme—Alberic—Stephen Harding

by
Jean-Baptiste Van Damme, ocso

Translated by
Nicholas Groves and Christian Carr, ocso

Adapted and Arranged by
Bede K. Lackner, O. Cist.

Cistercian Publications
Kalamazoo, Michigan – Spencer, Massachusetts
1998

Available from
Cistercian Publications (Distribution)
Saint Joseph's Abbey
Spencer, MA 01562

Cistercian Publications (Editorial)
Institute of Cistercian Studies
Western Michigan University
Kalamazoo, MI 49008

The work of Cistercian Publications
is made possible in part by support from Western Michigan University
to the Institute of Cistercian Studies

Printed in the United States of America

CIP Information available on request

TABLE OF CONTENTS

Preface   7

Introduction   9

Saint Robert of Molesme   17

Saint Alberic   53

Saint Stephen Harding   69

Epilogue   129

Select Bibliography   131

PREFACE

THE GREATNESS OF CÎTEAUX derives, without doubt, from the greatness of its three founders. Their example and work is an inspiration to every White Monk, and their ideals—the love of the cenobitic life, of Saint Benedict, the Rule, the brethren and the place—are the best guides for every *aggiornamento* in the great cistercian family. It would, therefore, be highly inappropriate to esteem only Saint Bernard's activities and the spiritual writings of their successor or to accept the argument that the early cistercian principles had already been discarded by the middle of the twelfth century.

While much has been written in recent years, on the basis of new evidence and brilliant insights, about the Founders' legacy, there was for a long time no modern historical work in existence which explored the first decades of the Order in some detail. This book by Jean-Baptiste Van Damme, ocso, a well known expert in the field, has set out to fill this gap. It examines the very origins of the White Monks through the lives of their saintly founders, in a thoughtful yet uncomplicated manner and should, therefore, be a welcome text to cistercian students and their friends, above all in novitiates and houses of study.

The French original of *The Three Founders of Cîteaux* made its first appearance in 1966. Sister Elizabeth Connor, ocso, Dr Nicholas Groves, Father Basil Pennington, ocso, and Dom Christian Aidan Carr, FSSC ocso, as well as a typist who in a true monastic fashion prefers to remain anonymous, devoted their time and considerable skill to translating it into English. They deserve the gratitude of all its readers now that, after long years, their dedicated labors have come to fruition.

The English translation tries—for obvious reasons—to remain faithful to the characteristics of the the original text. It reflects, therefore, the style and make-up of the latter in all aspects, including the comments, asides and monastic propaganda. It also wishes to be suitable for community reading whenever this may be desired. Some of the particulars may already be in need of updating, but since they have no direct bearing on the essential statements, no changes were made in the present edition and translation.

This book, although rich in content, is in essence only a survey; but it is also a work of love, as every such undertaking should be. It will hopefully lead to a more profound investigation of this all-important subject and inspire more detailed accounts about the formative and normative period of the Order for the benefit of all its readers. *Noblesse oblige!*

Bede K. Lackner, O. Cist.

INTRODUCTION

WRITING A BIOGRAPHY of the founders of Cîteaux is a difficult, if not impossible, task. The information transmitted by contemporary documents is insufficient to enable us to make an exact or remotely complete idea about their life and activities.

We have a life of Saint Robert in which we find several noteworthy facts written around 1220, at the time of his canonization, to make him known to a public interested in his cult. It does not, however, satisfy the most elementary demands of historical criticism. All its detail must be verified from other sources. The chartularies of Molesme and the documents contained in the *Exordium Parvum*[1] are the only texts that give us reliable information about him. The information about Robert we obtain from a collation of these two sources still leaves a wide gap in our knowledge, but the questions it raises incite further research: studies about the spirit and motives of his undertaking, his reform activities and the journeys he made in connection with the monastic movement of the eleventh century. The works we have just cited suggest that the foundation of the Cistercian Order, which an eight-hundred year-old tradition attributes to Robert, was indeed the fruit of his aspirations, but they offer no definitive evidence in favor of this thesis. Even so, the pre-history of Cîteaux and the life

1. *Exordium Parvum*, Introduction, in Van Damme, *Documenta pro Cisterciensis ordinis historiae ac juris studio* (Westmalle, 1959) p. 5. see also *idem*, 'Autour des origines', in *Collectanea Cisterciensia*, 20 (1958) 382.

of Robert's two successors as abbots of the New Monastery greatly help us comprehend the essential elements of his life, which was wholly devoted to the restoration of monastic discipline and of an authentic spirit and which culminated in the great cistercian reform as the natural outcome of his labors.

Our information about his successor, Alberic, is even more meager, but what we do know is valuable for rounding out the story of Robert and the origins of Cîteaux. Stephen Harding is better known to us, because of his life and his writings. These three men constitute a kind of trinity whose unity derived from their common ideal—an ideal they pursued with one heart and one mind in the same combat and selfsame enterprise. This was what their life was all about. Their individual contributions to this great spiritual construction constitutes the history of cistercian origins within the biographical triptych we present here.

This story is intimately connected with the general history of the period, which saw the growth of ecclesiastical and civil institutions and delicate connections between the Church and the secular powers at the turn of the eleventh and twelfth centuries. We shall first review these elements to understand the facts that surrounded the reform movement and the intentions which guided its authors.

Lay Investiture

We discover that the beginning of Robert's career coincided very nearly with the beginning of the Investiture Controversy and that the act which officially ended this conflict ran parallel with the completion of Cîteaux's establishment. 1050, the probable date of Robert's priorship in the abbey of Montier-la-Celle, is also the year when Saint Hugh (1109) began his abbacy at Cluny and the monk Hildebrand, named a councillor to Pope Saint Leo IX one year earlier, in 1049, began the fight against clerical abuses. This struggle grew, later, into a general reform movement which received its name from the monk-become-pope: the Gregorian Reform. In that same year, Anselm of Aosta became the prior and renowned school-master of the abbey of Bec, whose abbot he became in 1078 and which released him in 1093 to become archbishop of Canterbury. Finally, it was the year when Henry IV, emperor of the Holy Roman Empire and a fierce adversary of the Church's independence in the matter of investiture, was born. When his successor, Henry V, signed the Concordat of Worms in 1122, it had only been three years since official approbation had been given to the *Charter of Charity* by the same pope who had brought the conflict between Church and state to a successful conclusion— Callistus II (1118–1124).

We may wonder how the investiture of ecclesiastics by laymen, an abuse which led to many others, could have come into practice. In earlier days, bishops and abbots had conferred tithes, received from the goods of their churches, upon princes, knights, and nobles. These gifts compensated for services rendered to the Church or contributions to the expenditures of just wars, and we may also suspect that some of the more powerful lords had seized them by force or extorted them. To the possession of these goods was attached the obligation of supporting the priest in charge of the faithful living on the nobleman's domain, and this had as its consequence the involvement of the lay 'proprietor' in the appointment of clergy to the benefices. Little by little responsibility for these nominations fell to the lords, and whenever an abbacy or a bishopric fell vacant, they were, on the strength of their legal claims, able to influence the choice of candidate. In 962 Emperor Otto the Great was empowered by his protégé, Pope John XII, to designate the Roman pontiff; his successor, Henry II, around 1220 obtained the formal privilege of nominating bishops and investing them with the symbols of their authority. These practices became inalienable rights which were passed on to the heirs of the offices and benefices. Human weakness often exposed itself in the nominations and investitures: nepotism, family interests, bribery, intrigue, and politics were among the factors which determined the choice more than a concern for the spiritual welfare of the faithful laity, the monks, and the clergy. And whenever the appointees of the lords lacked in the strength, the virtue, or the talents to enforce discipline and provide for the formation of monks and priests, their weakness or bad example—not to mention the vice of simony which often lay behind their elevation to office—fatally brought with it loss of discipline in the monasteries and carelessness among clergy. But this state of affairs, widespread at all ecclesiastical levels in some areas, also aroused indignation and, in the long run, corrective reaction.

The Church and its supreme authority, the pope, had the means to reclaim what she had granted as a privilege and suppress what she had for long tolerated. The disorder introduced by these practices, with the complicity of her own ministers, impelled her to do just that. But the abuses were so deep-rooted that it seemed wiser not to pull the weeds too hastily, lest the good plants be destroyed. A thorough reform became imperative. To carry it into effect, it was necessary to rouse public opinion, create a vast spiritual movement, win over the leaders of the Church, and obtain the consent and willing cooperation of the secular authorities.

The Mission of Cluny

These reactions began with the foundation of Cluny in 910. Its purpose was the restoration of benedictine monastic discipline, by emancipating it from the control of secular lords, even though they had been its benefactors or the donors of its lands. The abbey, founded by Duke William of Acquitaine and Abbot Berno, was removed completely from lay control through the gift of its possessions to the Holy See. Its abbot could be appointed independently of any prince's or lord's preference. To assure the same liberty to the foundations emanating from Cluny, it was decided that Cluny would found only priories or 'cells' which would be wholly dependent on the central abbey. Priors would be nominated and replaced by the abbot at will. The monks would make profession into his hands. He would have full authority to assign or change their residence, while the goods would be administered and the revenues received by the abbey. Cluniac 'cells' were more dependent than the priories. They held only a small number of monks whose main function was to assure the abbey's presence in the scattered parts of its domain. At the beginning of Saint Hugh's abbacy the cluniac family had approximately sixty-five priories and 'cells'; by the time of his death, this number had risen to two-hundred directly founded or affiliated houses.

This rapid multiplication of foundations attests to the great generosity the lords showed the monasteries. For, mindful of their responsibility, they chose to give up properties whose ownership was at least doubtful and also other lands whose exploitation would help support the monks and contribute to a greater social progress through the work which this exploitation provided for the serfs and the new class of free workers. Raised on combat and far-flung expeditions, given to rough pleasures and exposed to the dangers created by privation and protracted absence from their homes, these knights and nobles were sincere Christians, anxious to repair their faults in order to escape everlasting punishments. The generosity of the lords was due to a love of justice and a respect for the rights of the Church and, in addition, to promoting religious interests to the welfare of society, which at this time had almost no source of livelihood other than agriculture. Socially and intellectually the leading centers of activity were the bishops', and the lords' courts, the *curiae*, and the abbeys. Most people lived from the cultivation of lands attached to the manors or farms of the ruling classes. They were compensated for their work but had to pay the tithe, according to the conditions of the land grant.

In addition to priories and cells, the powerful abbey of Cluny also attached already existing abbeys on the condition that their abbots would be nominated and, if need be, deposed and replaced by the lord abbot of Cluny. This was done to set up or safeguard their spiritual autonomy and regular observances.

A third way of associating monasteries with Cluny in order to support or promote monastic discipline was the introduction of the cluniac usages, or *Consuetudines*, into abbeys which were able and willing to maintain a good discipline; these abbeys preserved their economic, juridical, and moral independence. The total number of monasteries belonging in one way or another to the great cluniac family rose to about two-thousand.

In time, the *de facto* exemption of Cluny expanded through the granting of Roman privileges into a *de jure* exemption. Cluny became fully emancipated from secular influence and even from the authority of the local bishop. Its affiliated abbeys aspired to this same privileged status and did their best to attain it. After the beginning of the eleventh century, several among them were successful in this effort. The desire for *libertas* reverberated in monastic and spiritual renewal and found, therefore, an echo in Rome. Success achieved further inspired a similar zeal among the chapters and colleges of canons living in the shadow of cathedrals or collegiate churches.

In this way, a vast reform movement was taking shape. The Church, praying under the inspiration of the Holy Spirit to become once again her true self, discovered—in the souls of monks and canons—a saving potential, i.e., a spiritual mission which she was to wage against the control of the secular power. The renewal of evangelical fervor was more important to her than seeing her rights vindicated in the political arena, but, actually, both were necessary.

Monastic and Canonical Reforms

While the venerable institution of Cluny pursued its mission, new reform attempts appeared in the world of western monasticism. After a long career, Saint Romuald (1027) set down the fruit of his experience, studies, and struggles in the reform of Camaldoli, which attached the cenobitic life to eremitism. Saint John Gualbert (1073) similarly made several attempts to reform his monastery, but achieved the success in a fruitful and lasting reform only in a new foundation, Vallombrosa, which greatly resembled the reform of Camaldoli but had as distinctive characteristics the admission of lay brothers, the election of the abbot general, and uniform observances introduced on papal orders in 1090. At Fonte Avellana, Saint Peter Damian (1072) gave a new impulse to the eremitic life. In 1083, Saint Bruno founded the Chartreuse, setting up there a monastic life that was purely eremitical. Also in 1083, the pure cenobitism of Saint Benedict experienced a revival at Afflighem, foreshadowing Cîteaux in more than one respect. Grandmont, founded in 1076, set an example of poverty and independence from the secular lords by suppressing every external ministry, renouncing large animals, refusing properties beyond the enclosure and restoring manual labor—as all other monastic reforms had done. These decisions and sacrifices brought considerable material advantage to the populace and the clergy and earned the monks their goodwill and the affectionate nicknames 'poor brethren' and 'good men'.

By the middle of the eleventh century the canons joined the monks in the drive for a genuine and exemplary evangelical life. Their beneficial influence covered Provence, Romagna, Tuscany, and Lombardy and extended later, in the north, to the dioceses of Limoges, Paris and Reims; in the east, to Bavaria and Austria; in the south, to the Iberian Peninsula. Their main centers were Saint-Ruf in Provence, Saint-Quentin at Beauvais, and Springiersbach on the Moselle. The mature fruit of these reforms was Prémontré, founded in 1120 by Saint Norbert. The reforms of Saint-Victor and Arrouaise, near Arras, began shortly afterwards. Canonical reforms generally followed the regulations set up by the Council of Aix-la Chapelle in 816. It was probably because of the canons that the religious movement called for a return to the sources, they set out to recover the evangelical and ecclesiastical traditions contained in the canon of the councils, and even looked back to the *vita apostolica*, i.e., the life of the apostles and first Christians, and the authority of the Church Fathers, especially the legislators of the early canons and monks, Saint Augustine and Saint Benedict. To the renunciation of material goods and the total dedication of their lives to the service of the Gospel drawn from these ancient sources, they added such specifically monastic customs as manual labor, silence, and a number of practices taken from abbeys of monks. The canons of Prémontré, Saint-Victor, and Arrouaise were the first to borrow from the usages and constitutional laws of the Cistercian Order.

Like the canons, the monks spread into the Rhineland and Central Europe. The abbey of Gorze in Lorraine had an influence comparable to that of Cluny. But there things were quite different from what was prevalent in France. Gorze and a group of other benedictine abbeys had preserved the spirit of the reform of Aix-la-Chapelle (817). 'Cells' for instance, were unknown to them. Monasteries were autonomous; they were abbeys in the original sense of the word. But the complete independence that Saint Benedict had given his communities—aside from certain rights assigned to the local bishop—had been altered by bonds connecting these abbeys: they followed the same customs in matters that had not been regulated by the Rule: They sent death notices to each other and prayed for deceased confrères. They enjoyed a certain protection from lay lords and their discipline was controlled by common episcopal visitors. Gorze had neither the strict central-ization of Cluny nor the more flexible organization that Cîteaux was to introduce.

This picture should be completed with details on the struggle between the two universal powers in the political arena. They can be found in every general history of the Church. Let us mention several salient facts: the excommunication of Emperor Henry IV by Pope Gregory VII; the emperor's eventual deposition of the pope and nomination of an antipope; the exile of several popes; the resistance of bishops to charges of simony; the penance of emperors and princes; the meeting of councils and counter-councils; the captivity of Pope Paschal II, who was forced to renew the investiture privilege (which he revoked as soon as he recovered his freedom). These incessant struggles and countless difficulties did not stop the Church from pursuing an intense spiritual activity at every level. If the Founders of Cîteaux earned merits, they also had their share in the labors and sufferings that are the price of every victory.

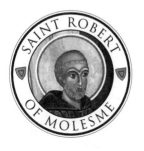

SAINT
ROBERT
of molesme

SAINT ROBERT OF MOLESME

T HE PLACE AND DATE of Robert's birth, as well as his family background and youth, are wrapped in mystery. Detailed studies have led historians to form theories which may be regarded as very probable. From the date of his death, which occurred in 1111 when he was in his eighty-third year, we are able to deduce that he was born in 1028 or 1029. His parents were Thierry and Ermengard, and they belonged to the family of the counts of Tonnerre, a branch of the Maligny. Accordingly, Robert was probably born and raised in the Tonnerrois or in Champagne.

Among the marvels that are said to have surrounded the birth of this blessed infant, there is one which interests the historian. While carrying this child, who was to play an important role in the kingdom of God and become an apostle of Marian devotion, his mother had an apparition of the Blessed Virgin who gave her a beautiful ring and told her that the child she would bring into the world was called to a spiritual espousal with her, the Queen of Heaven. This dream is only a legend, but it attests to an historical fact: the great renown of Robert's sanctity and the popular belief that he had a special vocation. Of his devotion to the Blessed Virgin we have only one direct and explicit testimony: the consecration of the church of Molesme to the Queen of Heaven and Earth and the very ancient law by which the Cistercian Order followed this example in all its foundations. Since Robert had laid the spiritual groundwork for the Order and this sign of his devotion to Mary was transmitted to posterity, he must be assigned the merit of having communicated to the Cistercian Order the cult of Mary, whose great herald was Saint Bernard. We should, however, note that on this point, as on a number of others, Cîteaux merely followed a tradition cherished by the great abbots and saints of the Cluniac world.

Beginnings at Montier-la-Celle

Since the call to monastic life coincided with his parents' desire that he take up studies, Robert embraced the religious life in the abbey of Montier-la-Celle. He entered, according to his *Vita*, at the age of fifteen. At some unknown date he became claustral prior, though it is generally believed that he was still relatively young when he was appointed to this office. His family background, his virtues, and his personal talents, as well as the local custom of appointing rather young abbots and priors, justify the hypothesis that the year 1050 was the probable date of this nomination.

At the time he held this office, a group of hermits was living at Colan, in a forest near the abbey. He himself had helped to found the group—an argument of devotion. And thus another legend based on the future evolution of this hermitage was born: that the foundation of Colan was the germ from which sprang both Molesme and Cîteaux. Very soon, these hermits received direction from a monk of Montier-la- Celle, but whether Robert added this charge to his priorship is not known.

Around 1068, at the earliest, the monks of Saint-Michel-de-Tonnerre elected Robert as their abbot. He agreed to this choice on one condition: that the monks accept the reform he considered necessary for their salvation. They promised, but did not keep their word.

At this point, the hermits of Colan asked Robert to become their leader, but in vain. Either because he disagreed with their eremitical way of life or because he felt obligated in conscience to continue the already–begun reform, Robert did not accede to their request A short time later he was obliged to leave Saint-Michel-de-Tonnerre and he returned to the monastery of his profession. The monks' lack of docility had left him no choice. The hermits renewed their request, but were again rebuffed.

The Foundation of Molesme

When the priory of Saint-Avoul-en-Provins, a daughter-house of Saint-Michel found itself without a superior, the monks requested and obtained Robert as their prior. But the hermits of Colan, refusing to give up, made one last attempt to attain their end. They appealed to the authority of the pope. The reigning pontiff was Gregory VII, a former monk and a zealous champion of monastic as well as church reform. He assented. This papal intervention, which shows that the pope shared the hermits' esteem for and their confidence in Robert, marks Robert's first contact with the leading monastic center of the eleventh century. Robert's name, already famous in his own region, from then on was also known in Rome. Unfortunately, we are not well informed about the details of this event and this gap also extends to the transfer of the hermitage of a new location—Molesme—in the following year.

The transfer no doubt had something to do with the situation and the location where the hermits had been living. Even though their resources had been adequate until then for maintaining one, then three, and finally seven monks, they could foresee that they would not be enough to support future members of the group. And, although the privations and hardships imposed by the circumstances of the place had been bearable for one man or a small group of men filled with a high ideal, they were likely in the long run to exceed the capacities of the growing numbers of recruits. Seeking a suitable location (*congruentiam loci desiderans*)[1] where they could establish themselves, Robert must have foreseen the establishment of a regular benedictine monastery, with a stream for

---

1. Kolumban Spahr, *Das Leben des hl. Robert von Molesme. Eine Quelle zur Vorgeschichte von Cîteaux* (Freiburg in der Schweiz: Paulusdruckerei, 1944) 11.

the needs of the kitchen, the mill, the laundry, and other facilities, and with nearby lands which could in time be made arable through the reclamation of the brushwood and trees.

Judged by its future success, the new location fully satisfied these expectations. But it also leads us to think that the intention to transform the hermitage into a regular benedictine abbey had been in Abbot Robert's mind and reform plans. Was this aspiration similar to the one plan he later conceived with Alberic, Stephen, and the other founders of Cîteaux? It is impossible to know: but it would be rash to deny it out of hand. Certain aspects of the foundation of Molesme foreshadowed the reform at Cîteaux and the establishment of the mother abbey of a new monastic order; but it would be difficult to see the essential points of the reform project of 1098 and 1100[2] in the reforming elements of 1075 and the following years at Molesme.

Still, there are a number of important similarities. We have already mentioned that, following the example of Molesme, all cistercian churches were dedicated to the Mother of God. Then, too we must remember that when Robert accepted the direction of the hermits of Colan, he wanted to impose a reform on them. He obliged them to give up the eremitic life to embrace the pure cenobitism of Saint Benedict; and the cenobitism of Saint Benedict was the specific objective of the cistercian reform.

Another detail should also be pointed out: the choice of an isolated, wooded and wild area. Manual labor did not frighten the founders in their zeal for poverty. The same resolve can be found in other contemporary reforms, especially those that issued from Molesme. The restoration of manual labor may have been part of the new foundation's program. But Cîteaux surpassed it in the demand it made in the realm of poverty and the esteem in which it held manual labor.

2. Jean-Baptiste Van Damme, *Autour des origines cisterciennes*, Extraits des *Collectanea Ordinis Cisterciensium Reformatorum* (Westmalle, Typis Ordinis Cisterciensis, 1958–1959) 79

Finally, let us note this important element: The domain of Molesme, which belonged to the lords of the Maligny, was given to Robert and his group as an allod, that is, it was not subject to rental obligations. The first Cistercians similarly strove to hold lands offered to them in this manner. In this way they could stay free of every inopportune contact with the world—such as having to put in an appearance in the courts and castles of the lords or being subject to the incessant comings and goings between abbeys and great land owners, or between the abbeys and their tenants of farmers, as would be necessary in the transportation of tithes. The Cistercians actually sought exemption from tithes; they wanted no longer to exploit the labor of their farmers and serfs in this way. But oftentimes they achieved complete success only after many years of waiting, numerous interventions, and repeated pleadings.

At Molesme, the domain had been donated absolutely, in frank-almoin; the monks were full owners and the donor retained no rights. An exception was made, however, for a group of serfs living on the estate of Molesme; they were allotted the land and supplied part of the tithe which this land paid to the church of Pouilly.[3] The property of Molesme had been donated by the Maligny family, the same family which had also endowed the foundation of Colan. This double donation leads us to conclude that the family was somehow related to Robert, the founder of both monasteries. The act of donation was signed by the principal donor, Lord Hugh of Maligny, and by his sisters and relatives. Tescelin the Red, the father of Saint Bernard, signed as a witness. The donation was made to Our Lady and the thirteen monks who pledged themselves to her service.

The Observance of Molesme

From the point of view of observances, one may be tempted to see in the foundation of Molesme a prelude to Cîteaux, a 'premature

3. Jacques Laurent, *Cartulaires de Molesme*, 2 vols (Paris: 1907–1911) 1: 115–116 and 2: 5–6.

Cîteaux', as some have written.[4] But, several reasons argue against this. In fact, Molesme lacked more than one essential element of the cistercian reform: for example, foundations which became true abbeys, the major importance accorded to certain points of the Rule regarding food, clothing, manual labor and the like, and the corollary institution of the lay brothers. On the other hand, the points it had in common with Cîteaux—solitude, flight of the world and love of poverty—can also be found in the other monastic reforms of the period. Still, it must be granted that the ideal of Molesme held in germ the ideal of Cîteaux and that the first cistercian house was an outgrowth of the former. The fact that one and the same man presided over both reforms supports this point of view.

Molesme was not yet Cîteaux. This becomes clear if one recalls the crisis of poverty it had to overcome around 1080. Between 1075 and 1079 the abbey lived in a poverty that was sometimes extreme. At times there was no bread. After a day of hard labor, the monks had nothing but vegetables to eat. In such circumstances no one would think to legislate about moderation in food or simplicity in clothing, as was later to be the case at Cîteaux.

The Growth of Molesme

One day the bishop of Troyes, Hugh II of Dompierre, passed through Molesme with a large retinue and was received with dry bread, the only nourishment the monks could afford at the time. The prelate was edified and deeply moved by this, and from then on maintained a generous friendship with them. He redoubled his generosity when he learned that, in spite of the gifts he had given them, they were obliged to go begging, even going as far as his episcopal city, to find relief. On the recommendation of the good bishop, the lords of La-Ferte-Loupiere donated to them arable lands and the churches of Flacy and Senan in the Senonais. These donations made possible the erection of priories bearing

4. *Ibid*, 1: 111ff.

these names. By 1081 at the latest, a priory had been founded at Vaucouleurs in the Champagne, on land granted by the lord of Joinville, Geoffrey II the Elder. At this same time, the priories of Radonvilliers, in the region of Brienne, and of Seche-Fontaine, in Bar-sur-Seine, came into existence. Expansion through the establishment of priories clearly shows that the model then in vogue was the cluniac regime. This institutional proliferation was accompanied by a growing spiritual radiation from the young abbey.

After the death of the bishop of Troyes, the monks' own bishop, Hugh Raynald of Langres, took it upon himself to care for the monks and to help them continue their expansion. In 1083 he appealed to the loyalty of his vassals and friends, authorizing them to donate churches and other ecclesiastical goods in their possession to the monks. Duke Odo I of Burgundy headed the list of benefactors. He gave the abbey a church located at Louesme in the Lassois, and it became yet another new priory. The number of daughter-houses had risen to eight by 1084, when Bishop Hugh Raynald died and was replaced by Robert of Burgundy, the duke's brother. The new bishop was to play an important role in the life of the saintly Founder, and the two Roberts died in the same year— 1111—as friends and brothers in Saint Benedict. Duke Odo was also to maintain close ties with Molesme, where he later held his feudal court on a number of occasions. And he was to be the donor and indispensable protector of Cîteaux in 1098.

The prestige of its benefactors explains the fact that by 1085 Molesme had become a rich and powerful abbey. The nature of the gifts demonstrates that the ideal governing before 1080 had given way to the customs of Cluny which disregarded manual labor as a means of subsistence in favor of an economy based on the acceptance of churches and the foundation of 'cells' and priories.

Holy Nostalgia

While the rhythm of foundations moved steadily ahead, a silent struggle began to unravel on the spiritual level. It was soon to erupt into public view and express itself for many years to come as a pressure for reform and the restoration of discipline.

The evidence for a relaxation of discipline is hazy but it all converges in a pattern that agrees with known facts. Robert's biographer denounced a scandalous relaxation of fervor; in speaking of the monks, he went so far as to say that 'Their hearts were overflowing with vices'. Here he apparently let himself be carried away by the temptation to heighten his account by borrowing a biblical expression from the psalms—in the belief, no doubt, that it was permissible to sacrifice objectivity for the pleasure of according a bit of relaxation to the reader, who was, in any case, accustomed to such a style. The *Summa Exordii*, or *Exordium Cistercii*, claims that although the monks of Molesme concerned themselves too little with the presciptions of the Rule of Saint Benedict, they never ceased to live 'in a saintly manner'. It explains the decline of discipline by the wealth which had been allowed to accrue to the abbey, and it praises poverty, the mother of all virtues, which is capable of producing men of strength. Poverty with its sister virtues had been expelled from Molesme after its increase in material goods. The *Exordium Parvum*, given its juridico-historical outlook, uses sombre phrases well-suited to its purpose, which was to formulate the real reason behind the cistercian reform: at Molesme, the monks did not observe the Rule they had professed. Finally, the *Exordium Magnum* lays the cause of the imbalance to mitigations which had been introduced over the centuries and legitimated by several councils, chiefly the synod of Aix-la-Chapelle in 817.[5]

Obviously, each of these documents contains a portion of the truth. To discern their real value and reconcile them, one must remember that Saint Robert had always been guided by a desire for regular observances and that this had spread by a sort of osmosis to part of his community. But at this moment, things had not yet

5. Spahr, *Das Leben*, p 13: Van Damme, *Autour*, pp. 139–140: *Exordium Magnum Cisterciense*, ed. Bruno Griesser (Rome: Editiones Cistercienses, 1961) 62: 'dum cottidianas regulae lectiones in capitulo audirent et aliud regulam praecipere atque aliud *consuetudines ordinis* tenere perpenderent . . .'.

reached the point they would by 1098. Before that happened, a considerable evolution, tied to historical circumstances, had to take place. We shall endeavor to describe its principal stages.

Saint Bruno and the Carthusians

A first, rather unique, reform attempt—for it had nothing in common with later reforms except certain circumstances of place and time—saw the light of day in 1082–1083. It was the successful attempt of Master Bruno of Cologne to found a new religious order.

Looking for perfect solitude where he could begin his monastic foundation, which was to combine the austerities of the desert with the advantages of the common life, Bruno turned to Robert of Molesme. This encounter was the beginning of a lasting friendship between the two men of God as well as a friendship between Robert and Bruno's disciple Lambert, the future abbot of Pothières in the vicinity of Molesme.

After Bruno had spent some time at Molesme, then in the throes of crisis, Robert placed the new priory or Seche-Fontaine at his disposal. With the help of several followers, Bruno began the construction of a small church and cells for the solitaries there. But since the new Order's economy was to be based on an indirect exploitation of its lands—which he could not hope to do successfully in the shadow of an abbey like Molesme, then in full bloom— Bruno quickly realized that he could not succeed in that place. Through the good offices of Abbot Seguin of la Chaise-Dieu, he obtained from the bishop of Grenoble the gift of an isolated area called Chartreuse. But Seguin had difficulties in persuading Bruno to accept this austere and remote wilderness. The site was so unhealthy, moreover, that after a few years it became necessary to move the monastery several miles further down the mountain, to the valley where the Grande Chartreuse is located today.

After his departure for the Chartreuse, Bruno made sure that the construction at Seche-Fontaine would be completed, for he wanted to hold on to the place for his hermits. His action shows how greatly he loved this solitude in the vicinity of Robert's abbey.

To the broad observance of Molesme and its frequent contacts with the world, the Carthusian opposed a rigorous seclusion which rejected every non-essential contact with the outside world. They adopted a poor and simple way of life devoted exclusively to prayer and silence. From the cluniac system they borrowed several elements: first of all, expansion through priories, which provided a stronger economic system for the central monastery and simplified the temporal administration of the daughter-houses; secondly, the exploitation of their arable lands by farmers. They refused gifts of churches and altars, for these would have entailed the obligation of exercising a ministry among the faithful.

The Hermitage of Aux

When Bruno took leave of Molesme and Seche Fontaine in 1083, the spiritual unrest fermenting in Robert's community burst into the open. Bruno's example must have influenced the more fervent cenobites. Some of them, including Robert himself, longed for the poverty and adherence to the Rule of the early years and pondered the restoration of the discipline of manual labor (in particular). The abbot tried to raise the spiritual level of his community, which adopted a rather easy lifestyle and had even fallen into certain abuses contrary to the recently introduced cluniac observances.

This regression is partly excusable. The repeated departures of swarms of monks to new priories under the leadership of resolute men could easily stifle the fervor of the thus impoverished community. Yet one fact above all must be kept in mind: the monks of Molesme had just exchanged their primitive austerities for the must less rigorous customs of Cluny. To step backwards to the past would have been extremely difficult for them. As they saw things, it was enough to adhere to the cluniac observance which was honorably followed in other monasteries—even though, in practice, they were unable to keep to it.

After a few years, Robert had to give in in the face of this impasse. Believing that his salvation was in danger, he joined a small group of hermits living at Aux, a place where the nuns of Jully were later to have a farm called Blanchevaux. The monks, of a carthusian cast, had introduced manual labor and by this modest means of subsistence, led a simple poor life in the ideal setting for virtue.

Back at Molesme, the abbot's absence had a very bad effect on progress and even on the maintenance of the abbey's spiritual and temporal life. His personality had lent prestige to the monastery in the eyes of its benefactors and other neighbors with whom he had had dealings on official occasions, as well as in the eyes of the neighborhood abbots, to whom he was bound by ties of friendship. The monks who did not choose to follow him in his attempts at reforming the observance (which he had nevertheless somehow managed to maintain at a relatively high degree of fervor), were still attached to him as a person and acknowledged his personal and spiritual greatness, even though it was too late. Encouraged by Bishop Robert of Burgundy, they went to the abbot to ask him to return to his monastery. But Robert saw his duty clearly and his conscience remained secure: he could not give up the life he had embraced after so much reflection and struggle, nor could he resume the charge of monks who had refused his patient, faithful pursuit of an authentic monastic ideal.

The monks, supported by their bishop, refused to give up; they solicited a papal order. The move turned out in their favor. A letter of Urban II (1088–1099) obliged Robert once again to take up the abbatial cross at Molesme. After an absence of approximately five years, the abbot returned to Molesme, probably in 1094. This was the second time a papal order had imposed a special obedience to Molesme on him. There would be yet a third.

These papal acts confirm the renown and esteem which Robert enjoyed among his sons and the lords of the region and help us to see the man through the eyes of his contemporaries: a real monk, a champion of the monastic life, and a true saint.

New Reform Attempts at Molesme

After returning to Molesme, Robert, still filled with zeal, set out once again to reform discipline. Soon several of his sons joined him in this effort. Among the most ardent was an English brother, Stephen, who enthusiastically embraced his abbots' views. Although relatively young—he may have been between thirty-five and forty at the time—he had had exceptional opportunities to enrich his knowledge and acquire experiences of the monastic life. We shall return to this later in discussing his abbacy. Destined by Providence to become abbot of Cîteaux and the organizer of the Cistercian Order, Stephen soon demonstrated that his enthusiasm was neither passing nor superficial. According to his compatriot William of Malmesbury, he was the first person to raise the idea of a foundation. This let us deduce that Stephen must early on have conceived a reform plan worth being discussed. William, who was Stephen's contemporary and may even have visited him, also claims that the general outlines as well as the specific details of his plan were debated by the community. This custom of consulting the community, in conformity with the Rule of Saint Benedict, was subsequently held in great honor.

Little by little, certain points of the Rule which had fallen into disuse were reintroduced. As the reform began, one of its first and most fervent champions was the monk Alberic, who was named claustral prior at Molesme probably in 1094 or 1095.

Robert's Journey to Flanders

At this point Robert undertook a long journey to Flanders. The fertile soil of this county, the industriousness of its people, the wisdom of its peaceful rulers and the christian charity practiced there all made the region a refuge for those in need. Robert went there in the hope of restoring his abbey's finances, which had been greatly compromised during his sojourn at Aux. The journey resulted in several donations of churches and other goods as well as the establishment of a new priory at Cohem in Therouanne.

Flanders too had important monastic centers. Robert doubtless came into contact with several abbeys, foundations, and reform attempts. He must have visited the abbeys of Saint-Vaast-la-Haut and Saint Martin of Tournai, which lay along his route: perhaps he even went as far as Afflighem. In any case, contacts between these three abbeys and the monastery of Cîteaux were later frequent. Of the monk-founders of Cîteaux, two were natives of Arras. Around 1124, Stephen, too, would visit the abbey located near that city.

By 1094, Saint Martin of Tournai followed, inspired by the same spirit as that soon to be found at Cîteaux: strict enclosure, poverty, the obligation of manual labor, the refusal of goods—like tithes—which were thought to belong by right to clergy and not to monks, the suppression of all superfluity in food and even in liturgy, the admission of lay brothers from all walks of life, the suppression of the house of nuns that had been started the previous year, and a preference for solitude, which keeps the monk from the clamor and distractions of the world. But Abbot Odo's excessive generosity and the failure of the monastery of nuns brought about a financial crisis which led to the abandonment of the scarcely begun reform and the resumption of the traditional observances. The experience would have given ample insight to anyone thinking about a reform of the monastic observance at the time.

The founders of Afflighem, under the influence of the itinerant preacher Werv, had also put into practice an *ordo monasterii* whose spirit bore a great resemblance to the spirit which a short time later inspired the reform at Cîteaux. They sought solitude, practiced almsgiving and hospitality, did manual labor to earn their living, and avoided luxury, even in the liturgy. The *Exordium Affighemense*, drawn up around 1122, not long after the *Exordium Parvum*, of Cîteaux, resembles the latter at a number of points. The two authors undoubtedly knew each other and the monk of Afflighem must have kept one eye on the work of his cistercian confrère and friend.

A Divided Family

At Molesme, while Robert was on his journey the discussions among the brethren about restoration of discipline and the eventual introduction of radical reform heated up and degenerated into squabbling. In time the tension between the two groups became so high that the opponents of a new observance, remembering an article of the Cluniac Customary that authorized them to use physical restraint against any disturber of the established order, seized, manhandled and imprisoned Prior Alberic.

This event, disedifying though it may be, must be seen in the light of the rough manners of the Middle Ages. People were used to violence. Even so, it reveals the inflexible opposition. The per-petrators of this violence entertained these arguments: when Saint Benedict sent his disciple Maur to Gaul, did he not authorize him to make adaptations which the food, clothing, climate, and customs of that country made necessary? Is the traditional adaptation to local conditions, which has been made by all the great monks, preferable to the practices of the Desert Fathers who fasted and did manual labor, not as a matter of principle but out of necessity? What is more, the opponents said, and it is imprudent to lay an unbearable yoke on people or a burden harmful to health, and it is iniquitous to make someone suffer in peacetime what the martyrs of the faith endured under persecution.

It proved impossible to convince these monks, most of whom knew only the customs of Cluny, that there could be a more perfect and more authentic benedictine life than the one they knew.

When he returned to his monastery, Robert tried to calm tem-pers. Although he favored reform, he realized he could not compel anyone, lest, in the word of Saint Benedict, being too zealous in removing the rust, he should break the vessel (RB 64). He allowed the two sides to co-exist. Even though they did not attack each other openly, the discord created uneasiness in the community. The family spirit was gone.

Aulps

In 1097, the reform movement experienced a solid gain. The cell at Aulps, which had been earlier founded by Molesme and remained its dependency, was raised to abbey status. The reason for this was the desire of the monks of Aulps to move on to a more faithful observance of the Rule of Saint Benedict. But the Rule does not know priories; in fact, it excludes them. On every page, it presupposes an abbot who leads the community as a father, who forms his sons in the monsatic life, and enjoys an autonomy limited only by the rights of the bishop.

Stipulations of the act still reflect the cluniac regime: the honors to be accorded the abbot of Molesme when he visits Aulps; his authority to correct and, if need be, depose his abbot-son and to replace him by choosing his successor from among the monks of the mother-abbey, and to reduce the abbey to the status of a cell if it were to become lax. All these details are patterned after the cluniac constitutional regime.[6]

But the rationale was heavy with meaning and rich in consequences. It contained in a way the germ of the future cistercian constitution and the principles of its reform. The intention to observe the Rule of Saint Benedict in its totality, combined with the rejection of priories, logically opens the possibility of a totally new life style based on the Rule and the expansion of an Order through the foundation of new abbeys.

We must realize that the system of priories was, in fact, not in harmony with the spirit of the Rule, for it was detrimental to monastic discipline. Leadership which, according to the Patriarch of western monasticism, must be both firm and paternal, requires a measure of autonomy and stability. The prior or superior of a cell, nominated or recalled by an absent abbot, could not know the sons

6. Laurent, *Cartulaires*, 2: 7–8: Van Damme, Documenta, 3

entrusted to him well enough to command their confidence and filial devotion. A monastic family is not a residence for missionaries. It presupposes regular, well-balanced and faithfully executed community exercises. The comings and goings between priories and cells, farms, courts, and castles, for the collection or payment of tithes, and the trips to the abbey of Cluny for professions and various temporal or spiritual transactions made stability and regular observances virtually impossible. In addition, the cluniac regulations imposed protracted psalmody and liturgical functions on the monks. Anyone who wanted to restore the benedictine life in its integrity had to attack the governance of Cluny and its observances. This was not an easy thing to do.

Founding an abbey was a difficult enterprise. By definition, an abbey had to be *sui juris*, that is, without any ties of dependence to its mother-abbey. No juridical bond could any longer existed between the mother-house and foundations, which could multiply. Even more: to be able to deal with secular benefactors and bishops in their own name, the new abbeys had to obtain a privilege from Rome. But, for Rome, the granting of privileges beyond the limits of the existing law, or in opposition to it, seemed a breech of good order and an obstacle to the preservation of discipline. In 1100, Paschal II forbade the elevation of priories to abbeys, in order to prevent the multiplication of isolated abbeys. A former cluniac monk, he must have been well aware of the concern an abbot of Cluny had for his daughter-houses. Aulps, erected before the accession of Paschal II, escaped this prohibition.

We should note one significant and enlightening detail: to the act which elevated Aulps, to abbey status, the three witnesses for Molesme were Abbot Robert, Prior Alberic, and Stephen, the secretary—the very group which was very soon to take the initiative in founding Cîteaux. This action, on a principle in direct agreement with their own reform plan, clearly represents a victory for them. It must have encouraged them to go ahead with their project but, at the same time, also have caused them to lose hope of bringing about reform at Molesme.

The First Official Step

It was under these circumstances and in this psychological atmosphere that the three future leaders of the reform, joined by four of their zealous companions, decided to go for permission to leave to Hugh of Die, archbishop of Lyons and permanent legate of Urban II. Why this appeal to the archbishop-legate? Not, of course, in order to withdraw from the authority of their own bishop, Robert of Burgundy, for shortly afterwards they were to make a foundation in the same diocese. It is possible they had earlier sought his advice. The sole reason was that several years earlier Robert had been recalled to Molesme by papal order; only the authority of the pope or of his legate could therefore annul that measure. The monks accordingly sought papal authorization from the legate to secede, for their enterprise had no chance of success at Molesme. Hugh wholeheartedly favored the gregorian movement; they knew this and were encouraged by it. Robert of Burgundy, the bishop of Langres, could have authorized the emigration of a group of monk-founders: he could not have allowed Robert to be one of them.

After listening to their hopes and difficulties, the legate was fully convinced that they could never implement their plans at Molesme. He advised the seven monks to leave the place and seek a new location.

Vivicus

Free to make a foundation, Robert did not go. Had his sons begged him to stay? Or did he prefer to send out a small advance group to prepare the buildings and grounds? Whatever the reason, he did not leave; instead four of his monks went to Vivicus. They were Alberic, Stephen, and two others whose names are not mentioned but their identity can be conjectured with great probability: on the list of the seven original petitioners Odo and John are mentioned between Prior Alberic and Stephen.[7]

7. Spahr, *Das Leben*, p. 15.

Their departure by no means pleased the opponents of the reform. They alerted the bishop, for Vivicus, like Molesme, lay in the diocese of Langres. The bishop listened to their complaints and requests and agreed to recall the founders. To add force to his order, he added the threat of excommunication for disobedience.

Why this appeal by the monks? And why the bishop's action? The brethren surely wanted to see the reform fail at any price. Informed by them, the bishop was bound to disapprove of Robert's absence. Even the intervention of the legate turned into a drawback, for the monks fell under his authority only because of Robert's presence. Had the abbot not been in the group, the bishop could have authorized them to make a settlement anywhere they wanted, away from Molesme.

The bishop also had the right to refuse them a site in his diocese. They had little choice but to obey. But having seen their resolve to embrace a more perfect life come to grief under his jurisdiction, they sought another means of carrying out their plan.

The Legate's Decision

The four founders of Vivicus returned to Molesme only long enough to talk with their abbot and to add to their group him and two other monks who had been present at the first audience. Then they made a second visit to the legate. Hugh was not at Lyons. They found him at some unidentified place, probably making visitations in his diocese. The matter suffered no delay. The legate gave them a friendly reception, listened to their explanation of the new situation, and sent them away, armed with the following letter:

> Hugh, Archbishop of Lyons and Legate of the Apostolic See, to Robert, Abbot of Molesme, and the brothers who with him desire to serve God according to the Rule of Saint Benedict.
>
> Be it known to all who rejoice in the progress of Holy Mother Church that you and certain of your sons, brothers of the monastery of Molesme, have stood in our presence at

Lyons and stated your wish to adhere henceforth more strictly and more perfectly to the Rule of blessed Benedict, which so far you have observed poorly and neglectfully.

But since it is obvious in view of many obstacles that this cannot be accomplished in the aforementioned place, we, providing for the welfare of both parties, those departing and those remaining, have concluded that it will be expedient for you to retire to another place, which Divine Providence will point out to you, and there serve the Lord in a more salutary and peaceful manner.

To you, therefore, who at that time presented yourselves— Abbot Robert and brothers Alberic, Odo, John, Stephen, Letaid, and Peter—as well as to all others whom you shall decide to add to your company according to the Rule and by common consultation, after due deliberation we issue the order that you persevere in this holy endeavor [and] we confirm this forever by the authority of the Apostolic See through the impression of our seal.[8]

The legate was happy to grant the request of Robert and his companions, whom he had twice received in audience. Having given the support of his authority, he was content with granting the permission they asked. He advised them to leave Molesme on the first occasion: on the second, he ordered them to do so. Far from evading responsibility in the matter, he obliged the monks to take this step by giving them a formal order to leave their abbey even before they had any idea of where they could settle. This radical measure was justified, first, by their duty to follow their conscience in leading a more perfect monastic life; and second, by the duly ascertained impossibility that they could put this ideal into effect at Molesme. Hugh did not merely take the side of those departing. He understood that he had a responsibility as well for

8. *Exordium Parvum*, ch. 2, in Van Damme, *Documenta*, 6. English translation by Bede K. Lackner, in Louis J. Lekai, *The Cistercians. Ideals and Reality* (Kent, Ohio: Kent State University Press, 1977) 451.

those who believed they were to remain in place. In practical terms, his decision amounted to a division of the community. Robert was to remain the abbot of the monks who left and those who remained were to elect a new abbot and profess their obedience to him, once they had been released from the vow which bound them to Robert. Those who left would remain obedient to Robert and merely transfer their vow of stability from the monastery and community of Molesme to Cîteaux and its new monastic family.

Robert and the Group of Founders

Robert's decision to join the founders did not have these changes of profession as its sole, even its chief, consequence. It also affected— and this is much more important—the whole future of the New Monastery and the new observance. Had Robert stayed at Molesme, the foundation would have remained under its mother-abbey either as a priory or, in the manner of Aulps, as a semi-autonomous abbey. This would have been a limping solution. If the monks were to succeed, they had to found an abbey that was fully *sui juris*. The necessity of founding abbeys to propagate their observance was later affirmed at the very beginning of their new constitution— which clearly indicates the fundamental importance of this statute and of Robert's presence among the founders. The legate had good reasons for giving the abbot an explicit order to join the group of founders.

Satisfied with the outcome, the seven monks returned to Molesme to give an account of the audience and to inform the community of the liberty that had been given to join them or to stay. The monks could reflect on the vow they had taken to observe the Rule faithfully and on the guarantees which the legate's authority offered them for fulfilling this obligation. They could see that the prelate had taken a personal interest in the reform and entrusted its leadership to their abbot. Fourteen other members of the community decided to join the founders.

So they departed, twenty-one in number. With them they took only what was strictly necessary in liturgical furnishings and books.

Devoid of all material aid, they had nothing but their trust in Divine Providence.

The Problem of Dates

Here we must pause to take a look at the rather thorny problem of dates. The year in which Aulps was raised to an abbey is stated in the act: 1097. The same document, however, is also dated to the fourth indiction.[9] This seems to conflict with the other date, for it refers to the year 1096. The indiction—and this has escaped several authors—begins not with the beginning of the year, but on 25 September.[10] The fourth indiction refers to the year which elapsed between 25 September 1096 and 24 September 1097.

The act also gives another point of reference. It is dated to the ninth year of Urban II's pontificate; this ran from 12 March 1096 to 11 March 1097. Hence, the act must be dated to the period between 25 September 1096 and 11 March 1097. But, because the year—1097—is given, we have to conclude that the event took place before 11 March 1097, but after the preceding Christmas, (December 25), for the data can be reconciled only if we assume that we are dealing with the roman or papal indiction, which begins the year on 25 December (or the 1st of January).

This conclusion is confirmed by the date of Cîteaux's foundation, which is similarly established with the help of two references that can be reconciled only if we admit the same indiction. The *Exordia* date the foundation at the 1098th year of the Incarnation, while the *Exordium Magnum* places it exactly on the 21st of March and Palm Sunday—a detail which only can be true if we are dealing with a roman (papal) indictment.

The sojourn at Vivicus lasted for some time, for Robert's *Vita* mentions that the four solitaries were driven from it *aliquanto*

9. A period of fifteen years. When completed, the cycle began again with the initial unit.

10. The roman or papal indiction, which is still used today in papal bulls, begins on the first of January, but here we are dealing with the imperial indiction which began on 25 September.

tempore. This expression could mean several months after their arrival, which must have occurred in the fall of 1097, or at the beginning of the following winter. Thus, one must calculate that approximately one year passed between the elevation of Aulps and the departure of the twenty-one monks from Molesme.

As for the two meetings with the archbishop-legate Hugh: the first must have taken place in the spring of 1097; the second, in the winter or early spring of 1098.

A Group of Benefactors

The legate's protection had the additional advantage that, at his intervention, Robert and his monks received considerable help from Duke Odo I of Burgundy. The duke had already shown his goodwill toward Molesme in 1085, on the recommendation of his brother Robert, who had just been named bishop of Langres. This gesture on his part was quite remarkable, for he never or rarely showed any interest in abbeys. His interests lay in riches and exploits and—when there was no opportunity for combat—in periodic rampages with his soldiers, and he had no qualms about ransacking traveling bishops or abbots.

One day in 1097, Odo learned that the archbishop of Canterbury, Saint Anselm, was passing through the duchy on his way to Rome. Hoping for rich spoils, he went after him to plunder his possessions. A great surprise awaited him. The modesty, poor trappings, affability and admirable manners of Anselm wholly confounded him. He immediately begged the saintly prelate's pardon, promised assistance and protection, and had his party escorted to the frontier of his duchy.

On his return, the english archbishop was the guest of Hugh of Lyons. The resignation Anselm had submitted from the pope had not been received, and he had to wait for a favorable opportunity to return to Canterbury. He enjoyed the legate's hospitality for quite some time and must have been at Lyons in 1098, when the first Cistercians made their foundation.

Another prominent churchman also used his influence to promote the monks' cause: Archbishop Guy of Vienne, the son of

Count William the Bold of Burgundy and the brother-in-law of the duke who married his sister Matilda. William of Malmesbury, writing around 1120, confirmed this in the following words: 'There [at Cîteaux] they began their admirable work with the support of the archbishop of Vienne, who is now supreme pontiff.' Guy of Burgundy continued to be a friend and protector of the Cistercians until his elevation to the Apostolic See and, as we shall see, even after his death.

To round out our report about the friends and benefactors of the foundation, we must mention finally the Viscount of Beaune, one of the first donors and in all probability a member of Robert's family.

Abbot Robert obviously approached this group of friends. According to two seventeenth-century cistercian historians, Bernardo Brito[11] and Angelus Manrique,[12] he was accompanied and assisted by Stephen, who, as we already know, was his secretary and who because of his nationality may also have attracted the attention of Anselm of Canterbury. Both historians print the text of two letters, one of them addressed to the duke and thought to have been written by Stephen in his abbot's name; the other the duke's purported reply. But the two letters cannot be considered authentic. Their style and the titles employed in them do not agree with the practices of the late eleventh century. The content of the duke's letter, promising to win over the pope and the bishops of the duchy to Robert's cause, is wholly unlikely for, according to the official account, it was instead the papal legate and the bishops who asked for the duke's help.

The Foundation

The principal and most important temporal benefactor of the foundation was the Duke of Burgundy, Odo I. He persuaded his vassal, Viscount Raynald of Beaune, to cede to the monks

---

11. Bernardo de Brito, *Chronica de Cister . . . Primeira parte* (Lisbon, 1602).

12. Angel Manrique, *Cisterciensium seu verius Ecclesiasticorum Annalium a condito Cistercio . . .* 4 volumes (Lyon, 1642–1659).

a tract of land being newly cleared at a place called Cistellum. This land, a portion of the patrimony of Hodierna, the viscount's wife, was an allod, that is, a property free of any feudal obligation. In a first deed, Raynald ceded an area large enough to allow the construction of the regular buildings and outbuildings and as much arable and untilled land as the monks needed for their livelihood. A second deed confirmed the first and enlarged the donation by giving up any and all claim to a chapel already on the site. The monks refused the gift of the church, thus avoiding any implicit recognition of a layman's right to possess or to donate churches. Accepting this gregorian view, Raynald declared that he had no right over this sanctuary which, he now claimed, belonged to God alone—thus allowing the monks to take possession of it as if they had been its original owners (*primi occupantes*). The donation was completed by a third act which ceded an entire allod to the monks and requested that one strip of arable land be left to the use of two male and one female serfs. The tract needed for the monks' livelihood was to be designated by the viscount, by Lady Hodierna (if she wished to concern herself with it), and by Abbot Robert, and it was to be at a good distance from the lands cultivated by the monks. The three serfs were to remain subject to the viscount, not to the monks, who would certainly have refused any stipulation of this kind as contrary to their principles. This enlargement of the original donation was actually the work of the duke who had obtained it from the viscount by offering him in compensation an annual rent of twenty *sou* (gold *solidi*) and by giving permission to him and his heirs to plant as many vineyards on their domain as they could cultivate.

All these donations were confirmed, as required by Church law, by the hand of the local bishop, Walter of Chalon, on the day the church was dedicated. On the same day Odo made a new grant, giving full permission to the monks to fish, hunt, pasture and cut wood on lands he held adjacent to the abbey. Taken together, these measures assured the monks the peaceful possession of their privileges, exemption from any secular encroachment, and perfect tranquility—indispensible conditions for a life devoted exclusively to God according to the Rule of Saint Benedict.

Inexhaustibly generous, the duke made yet another donation to the New Monastery—the name given at the foundation—in the form of animals, building material and whatever else was necessary for the completion of their wooden buildings. He also assumed responsibility for all their needs for a long time to come.

The exact dates of the dedication of the chapel and the erection of the monastery into an abbey are not known. The two ceremonies, presided over by the bishop, may have taken place on the same day, for the chapel was already there when the founders arrived. The occasion may also have coincided with the bishops confirmation of the donations. All these official acts could not have been delayed long after the monks' arrival at Cistellum, for the abbot had to be canonically installed by his ordinary and the monks had to vow stability to the new place and community without delay.

One last event marked the foundation. On Christmas Day, 25 December 1098—the only Christmas Robert spent at Cîteaux[13]—the duke made an important donation to Robert: a vineyard located at Meursault. Soon afterwards the Founder was to be asked to give up the place which fulfilled his lifelong aspiration and to accept being separated from the sons who had shared his ideals, his joys, and his sorrows.

New Crisis at Molesme

While the foundation was moving forward, the founders' former confrères at Molesme elected a new abbot and daily life went along in the traditional manner. The two communities seemed fully resigned to the division enacted by the legate. But the peace did not last long: it was broken in a way no one had apparently foreseen.

While the Cistercians were enjoying the favor of the magnates, prelates, and lords, and their life being admired, their temporal

13. Jean Marilier (ed.), *Chartes et documents concernant l'Abbaye de Cîteaux, 1098–1182* (Roma: Editiones Cistercienses, 1961) nn. 4–12, pp. 36–38.

security clearly assured, and their spiritual life heartened by the entrance of a large number of postulants, Molesme, once a rich and powerful abbey, saw its prestige decline because of the departure of its saintly abbot and several of its members outstanding in virtue, talents, and illustrious birth. This had a disheartening effect on the monks and greatly upset their neighbors and benefactors. Donors may have lost confidence in the new management of the abbey's goods. Perhaps the tithes they received from Molesme fell below their expectations. They spoke derisively about the abbey and became increasingly hostile toward it. One of them, Count William II of Nevers, swayed by rumors or simply anxious to exercise his' right of arson'—a form of extortion accepted as legitimate—burned down one of the abbey's dependencies. This was like throwing a stick into a flock of hens; it brought instant and widespread attention to what was happening.

The monks of Molesme claimed they had been unjustly treated by their confrères and blamed them for their misfortunes. As if to avenge themselves and turn the ridicule from themselves, they seized every opportunity to revile and annoy them. To restore good order in their monastery and peace with their neighbors, and thus also recover their material prosperity, they asked the bishop to use his full influence to restore their abbot Robert to them. As we will see later, they also hoped to destroy the reform, for they had certainly realized by then that without Robert's leadership it would be in great danger. But the bishop, the brother of the recently converted duke who had taken a great interest in the foundation, was not about to cooperate in any reversal of the work under way, especially as this have would also have meant going against the decisions of his archbishop, and the papal legate. At the same time he had to save Molesme at any price and risk bold action.

The only chance of success lay in appeal to Rome. In spite of his kinship with the duke and his subordination to the legate, Bishop Robert of Burgundy supported the initiative of the monks, who selected two or perhaps several of their number as delegates. These representatives arrived around Easter, which in 1099 fell on

16 April. On the 24th of April a synod was convened, chaired by Pope Urban II. Giving a detailed description of their unhappy situation, the monks of Molesme insistently begged the pope and the cardinals that Robert be returned to them as abbot.The pope himself bore witness to their unusual pleading when, in writing to his legate, he remarked that they had reclaimed their abbot with considerable vehemence (*vehementius*). He added, as if to excuse himself to the legate, that he was obliged and even constrained (*coacti quidem*) by his brothers, the cardinals, to grant them a favorable hearing. He invited the legate to investigate the possibility of Robert returning to Molesme and, if it was feasible, to ensure that it happened. At the same time the legate was to see to it 'that those who love solitude [Cîteaux] may live in peace, and those who are in the monastery [Molesme] observe the regular discipline'.[14] In the face of this reserved and somewhat diffident papal attitude, the legate judged it unwise to assume responsibility in the matter. He, even more than the pope, had reasons to be apprehensive about the reactions of the offended party. He therefore summoned a council of *viros authenticos*, that is, important persons in official positions, to discuss the measures to be taken.

The Meeting at Port-d'Ansell

According to the official report, the meeting was held at Port-d'Anselle.[15] Several bishops and religious superiors attended it. One of the most directly interested dignitaries, Robert of Burgundy, the bishop of Langres, did not. Why was he absent? No document tells us. Since his absence is, to say the least, surprising, may we assume that he felt slighted at not having been allowed to resolve this problem, which under normal circumstances would have fallen under his authority? Having previously managed to effect Robert's return from the foundation of Aux, moreover, he

14. *Exordium Parvum*, chs. 5–6; Van Damme, *Documenta*, 7–8.
15. *Exordium Parvum*, ch. 7; Van Damme, *Documenta*, 8–9.

may have been afraid that requesting the same favor a second time from the same pope would meet with refusal. Even if papal and legatine interventions were proper from a canonical point of view, Robert may have felt slighted at having the matter referred to the court of the legate whom he had bypassed in appealing directly to Rome. He was content to be represented by Godfrey, the new abbot of Molesme, and by several monks of the abbey who were as interested as, indeed more interested than, he in resolving the case and equally capable of presenting an exact account of their situation and making a convincing plea. The assembly must have met in May or early June of 1099; the legate could have received the papal letter only after the Roman synod which was held at the end of April. The pope who had written it died on 29 July, and on that day every commission, including Hugh's legatine office, automatically came to an end. One of the decisions taken at Port-d'Anselle was that a breviary which had been taken along from Molesme by the founders was to be returned to that abbey by the feast of Saint John Baptist, 24 June. If the breviary was not to be returned until 24 June 1100, this would have been specified in the decree: besides, the delay would have been too long. On the other hand, the interval between the synod and the feast of Saint John 1099 seems rather short, but not too short if the scribes worked as a team. One monk could prepare the parchment, another mark the lines of the margins and spaces, a third ready the ink, a fourth trim the pens, and so on.

Robert's Return to Molesme

At the meeting at Port-d'Anselle Robert's fate was decided: he was to return to Molesme. A report sent to the bishop of Langres describes the discussion and its outcome. This valuable document also helps us reject the biased accounts several authors have given of Robert's behavior. Misled by national prejudices or by rumors of petty jealousies among the monks, some medieval and modern writers have accused the founder of Cîteaux of weakly and cravenly failing to discharge his obligations toward his sons and toward God. To those who judged him this way, the meeting at Port-d'Anselle was, so-to-say, Robert's trial. It is easy to demonstrate that these accusations are without serious foundation.

Before the panel, composed of the legate, several bishops and abbots and other prominent persons of the region, appeared the monks of Molesme, led by their abbot Godfrey, who had been elected after Robert's departure to Cîteaux. Their bishop was absent, having contented himself with a written recommendation which the monks handed to the legate. Their common request was urgent and allowed but one solution: that Robert be obliged to return to Molesme. Since the alternative left open by the pope was clearly unworkable, the parties themselves discarded it in favor of the only possible solution. Abbot Godfrey declared himself ready to relinquish his office to Robert.

Having listened to the monks' report and re-read Urban II's letter, the legate and his advisers decided that they must resign themselves to the facts and the situation. They therefore granted the monks' request: the return of their abbot. But they did so on the condition that Robert renounce all his rights over Cîteaux: the pastoral staff of Cîteaux was to be returned to the bishop of Chalon. This symbolic gesture meant that Cîteaux would remain an abbey and that the bishop, in accordance with canon law, would preside over a new election. In the meantime, Bishop Walter would free Robert from obedience to himself and his diocese, and Robert would in turn release the monks of Cîteaux from the vows which bound them to himself. Those among them who expressed the desire to do so were given the freedom to return with their abbot and become members of the Molesme community once again. Finally, it was agreed that from that time forward there would be no further transfers between the two abbeys, except in the manner prescribed by the Rule, as these things were always done between independent abbeys.

The legate had once again saved the reform, this time by preserving the abbatial status of the new foundation. Thenceforward it would exist alongside Molesme, but without any tie of dependence. It was also stipulated that if Robert should ever again leave Molesme *solita levitate*—as had happened more than once before—then Godfrey would resume his office, unless the legate, the bishop, or Abbot Godfrey decided otherwise.

With his apostolic authority, the legate ordered the bishop of Langres to receive Robert with courtesy and reinstall him as abbot. Although the bishop had not requested it, this order was issued in writing, for the procedure which had been followed was not the ordinary one and had received its force from the supreme authority of the Church as represented by his legate. The liturgical books and ornaments which had been taken along from Molesme, it was decided, would remain at Cîteaux except the breviary mentioned earlier.

Bishop Walter of Chalon and Abbot Robert did as the legate had ordered. Robert and several of his sons returned to Molesme. He had no choice, and there can be no doubt that the separation caused him great distress. He was taken from the work that crowned his constant efforts and from those of his sons who had best understood him and shared his struggles, sufferings, joys, and hopes. Those who returned with him to Molesme made use of the liberty that had been given them, because they did not find the desert to their liking. Robert's presence likely played a role in their decision, but one cannot ascribe to him a lack of love for the desert. Nothing in his conduct or in any document justifies such an interpretation of the facts or of his conduct.

Behind the foundation of Cîteaux, as we have already seen, lay the conscientious duty its monks felt to live according to the Rule of Saint Benedict, according to their profession. It could, therefore, be objected that if Robert was mindful of this duty in leaving Molesme for Cîteaux, then his return constitutes a condemnation of his conduct. By leaving the place where he knew he ought to live in accordance with his profession, he made himself guilty of perjury. In truth, however, the law which authorizes the espousal of a more austere life must yield to the law of necessity if there is a clear conflict between the two obligations. The synod of Port-d'Anselle had publicly and solemnly stated that such a necessity existed for the monks of Molesme, and the decision taken at it had been made by common accord and confirmed by the apostolic authority invested in the papal legate.

The account as we have given it, wholly consonant with the documents and the spirit which inspired these events, lets us reject as false the accusation of disobedience levelled against Alberic and his three companions who had for some time lived at Vivicus.

Here we must pause to take a brief look at the mordant expression, *solita levitate*, which was inserted into the report. Abbot Godfrey willingly relinquished his place to Robert, it states, and then goes on to say: but if with his usual inconstancy Robert should again leave his post, no one shall be put in his place without the prior consent of the legate, the bishop, and Godfrey. These words undoubtedly refer to Robert's numerous relocations, that is, to the readiness with which he always obeyed the inspirations of grace and the orders of his superiors. He had just been given a new order which, through the legate, went back to the pope: he was to give up his stability at Cîteaux. This was the third papal order obliging him to return to Molesme. His inconstancy was not a blameworthy fault which the legate denounced, but a quality he appreciated in Robert. He used a figure of speech suited to the literary taste of his time. To him Robert's inconstancy, like the mobility of the angels, was simply a readiness to go wherever obedience called him. The prelate knew that he was utterly faithful to his obligations and obedient to the injunctions of his superiors. He was to give proof yet again of this docility We might also add that Hugh may have wished to be diplomatic, either to free himself from any blame he may have incurred or else to break the tensions and thus help those who had been suffering from this rather tragic situation. In any case, he had to consider the possibility that Robert might once again return to Cîteaux, because his mission at Molesme had either failed or come to an end once he had restored order and groomed a capable successor.

This battle of procedures inspired one final document: Robert's dimissory letter, given by the ordinary of Chalon to his colleague at Langres.[16] The author of the *Exordium Parvum* calls it a 'shield of defense' (*scutum defensionis*), a biblical turn of phrase dear to medieval writers. We may be astonished to read at the end of this letter: 'Do not be afraid to accept him and to treat him as a man in good standing'. This clause does not suggest that Robert had been cleared of some reproach which he may somehow have deserved. We need only recall the efforts of the bishop of Langres, Robert of Burgundy, both at the court of Rome and later at the synod of Port-d'Anselle, at first to keep Robert at Molesme and the second time, to make him return there. He could only be happy to see Robert return to Molesme and his jurisdiction and edified by his submission.

Several other details emerge from the report of the meeting addressed to the same bishop of Langres. Liberty was given to those who had followed Robert to the 'desert' to return with him if the new life was too difficult for them. 'Several' (*quidam*), says the *Exordium Parvum*, took advantage of this permission, because 'they did not find the desert to their liking'. Occasionally, this reproach has also been applied to Robert: William of Malmesbury claims that Hugh's councillors 'compelled the writing [Robert], *volentem cogentes*.[17] The *Exordium Parvum*, the only authentic source but one which William seems to have ignored, does not allow this interpretation. When speaking of Robert, it says that upon the formal request of the pope and the counsel of persons worthy of trust, the legate announce: 'We have decided to return him because the monks who had been asking for him had no hope of seeing peace and tranquility restored in the monastery of Molesme in any other way'.[18]

16. *Exordium Parvum*, ch. 8; Van Damme, *Documenta*, 9.

17. William of Malmesbury, *De gestis regum Anglorum libri quinque*; PL 179:1289 B.

18. *Exordium Parvum*, ch. 7; Van Damme, *Documenta*, 8.

Which and how many monks returned with Robert to Molesme? The term *quidam*, given the total number of twenty, could mean half a dozen. For a lesser number the author would have used *aliqui* or *pauci*. If half of the community had been involved, one would expect *plures*. Among these returning was Peter, a friend of Stephen Harding, and also English by birth, who later became chaplain to the nuns of Jully and attended Bernard's sister Humbelina on her deathbed.

At the end of the report the legate named the persons who had been present in the deliberations: the bishops of Autun, Chalon, Macon, and Belley; the abbots of Tournus, Dijon, and Ainay; the pope's chamberlain, named Peter, and several other 'upright persons of good repute'.

This was the second time that Hugh of Die, who was more Gregorian than Gregory himself, had saved the reform. The future seemed assured, thanks chiefly to the legate's sure and unwavering protection. Even so, the peace established by the prelates' arbitration and the legate's decision was not to last long.

On the following July 29th, scarcely two months after these measures were taken, Pope Urban II died and Hugh's mandate came to an end. The right moment had come for the monks of Molesme to resume their attempts to destroy the reform which both humiliated and scandalized them. Hugh was still there as archbishop of Lyons, however, and others were soon to enter the scene to continue the struggle and provide for the stable and unassailed existence of the foundation.

Twilight of a Saintly Life

Robert was seventy years old when he took up the abbatial cross at Molesme once again. During his twelve remaining years, he undertook remarkable activities and raised his community to great renown. A notice from 1105 gives us the following testimony: 'The good odor of the renown of the monastery of Molesme is recognized far and wide. The lords shower it with gifts and ask its monks to make new foundations in their midst'.[19] Within a short time, the abbey's influence extended as far as Luxembourg, where the priory of Ueseldingen sprang up, and in the dioceses of Basle and Lausanne, where foundations were made.

Among the numerous transactions in which Robert or his monastery were involved, we must mention the elevation of a former 'cell' to the rank of an abbey and the agreement concluded between Molesme, her daughter Aulps, and Aulps' daughter Balerne. In 1107, at the latest, an act was drawn up between Duke Thierry of Lorraine, Bishop Pibo of Toul, and Abbot Robert, raising the monastery of Chatenois in the diocese of Toul to an abbey at the duke's request. That the new abbey was to be independent of Molesme was expressed by a symbolic gesture of the new abbot: he received the pastoral staff, not from any prelate or prince, but from the altar. He and his government were to be under the vigilance and jurisdiction of the bishop and the abbot of Molesme.[20]

In 1110, the *Concordia Molismensis* was drawn up: to this we shall return when discussing Stephen's abbacy.

Robert died in the Lord on 17 April 1111, after a life of unceasing struggle and immense labors. Through his great zeal he acquired numerous merits which he deployed on behalf of a truly fervent monastic life.

19. Laurent, *Cartulaires*, 1: 152, 11.
20. Laurent, *Cartulaires*, 2: 126–127.

sAiNt
AlbERic

SAINT ALBERIC

WHEN HE RETURNED to Molesme, Robert left at Cîteaux a community which may be described as fairly prosperous. The temporalities were so well assured that the monks, leading a life of voluntary poverty, did not suffer any privation. The decrease of the community caused by the departure of Robert and some of the co-founders, was compensated for by the entry of a good number of postulants, as we shall soon see. The monastery, made of wood—probably with a stone cellar—had to suffice for their immediate needs, but a transfer of their residence would become necessary in the near future. The scriptorium, while contributing to a spirited monastic life, had certain needs. An important mission, modest resources, and a young community filled with zeal—this is what awaited the successor of the founder and first abbot of Cîteaux.

Under the direction of Bishop Walter of Chalon, the monks elected to this office their former prior Alberic, 'a man of great learning, well-versed in both the divine and human sciences, and a lover of the Rule and of the brothers'.[1] This assessment in the *Exordium Parvum*, no matter how laconic, is substantive. It is practically the only direct reference we have to Alberic as a person, but it well describes the important role he was destined to play. The abbey and the Order of Cîteaux owe him a great deal both spiritually and temporally. Under his direction, the new

---

1. *Exordium Parvum*, ch. 9; Van Damme, *Documenta*, p. 10.

observance was to take its first steps. And while it is true that the establishment and organization of daughter-houses would be left to his successor, it was incontestably Alberic who provided their 'practical' foundations, what may be called the setting-in-motion, the years of experimentation, of the cistercian reform.

Abbot Alberic

Nothing at all is known about Alberic's background. Since the official account of the origins of the Order specifically says that his successor, Stephen, was English by birth, but never mentions Alberic's nationality, we may assume that he was a native of the region, or perhaps of the Longonais, Champagne, Burgundy and even Lorraine.

From various details of his life we may conjecture on the approximate date of his birth. He died in January 1108, apparently without having reached a very old age, and he was in the group that had founded Molesme in 1075.[2] We may therefore place his entry into religion at roughly 1070. And since he had a reputation for learning, he must have received his intellectual formation prior to that year; this suggests that he was about twenty-five years old when he entered. The date his birth can be assigned, with great probability, somewhere between 1040 and 1050.

His years of formation in both sacred and secular knowledge were marked by the influence of Lanfranc, the teacher of genius who directed the abbey school of Bec from 1045 to 1060. Even if Alberic did not attend his classes, he came under his influence in whatever schools he did attend; the most important schools of the day were Reims, Chalons-sur-Marne, Chartres, and Paris.

On becoming abbot, Alberic had to instruct his sons in sacred learning, serve as a model in the pursuit of perfection, and take good care of the temporalities of his monastery. Running the scriptorium gave him an opportunity to prove his mettle. The artistic and intellectual output of this monastic workshop reveals the skills and talents of the man who organized it. A letter of Lambert, abbot

2. Spahr, *Das Leben*, p.17.

of Pothières, addressed 'to Alberic and his brethren', suggests that the abbot shared its work and that his group of copyists and scribes enjoyed an excellent reputation. The document starts with this very flattering admission:

> By writing to me in the hope of being cured of your ignorance by an unlearned man, you might appear to have acted out of irony rather than a desire to learn, were your very life not a testimonial to righteousness. For, if I may use a proverb, you have sent a lamb to get wool from a goat! You are asking a poor worn-out man, a dotard stricken with lethargy and stammering with toothless mouth, to teach Minerva herself.[3]

We shall have another opportunity to talk about the scriptorium, particularly in connection with the work of Stephen Harding. In dealing with Alberic's abbacy, we will look at the initiatives he took to strengthen the juridical and material foundations of his institution.

Consolidation of the Reform

First, let us look at the reform program. This must be seen as the fruit of the collaboration of all the founders, especially the three leaders. Alberic has the merit of having given it its definitive form and obtained approval for it from Pope Paschal II.

The guiding principle of the reform was the founders' intention to live according to the Rule of Saint Benedict by giving up traditions and customs introduced over the centuries. This resolve weighed heavily on the consciences of these fervent men, who were convinced that realization would assure perfect fidelity to the prescriptions of the Rule. The obligation of conscience also provided a valid juridical reason for creating a new observance and establishing an independent monastery and later a new monastic order.

Moving from this principle to concrete applications, they decided to suppress all clothing and food not recognized by the Rule and to reject, even in the liturgy, everything contrary to the will of

3. Marilier, *Chartes*, n. 17, pp.41–46.

their holy Legislator. Entering into the spirit of the Rule, they also renounced forever such 'easy' sources of income as churches, altars, tithes, ovens, and mills, and they prohibited the entrance of women into the monastery. In all this they followed the example of Saint Benedict, who foresaw no means of subsistence other than manual labor. These measures also had the advantage of ensuring solitude and forestalling litigation with other persons interested in the same goods. The monks justified their conduct by appealing to the authority of the Church Fathers, who had assigned ecclesiastical revenues to four groups of people: the bishop, the parish priest, the guests, and the poor.

This uncompromising choice of a life of strict seclusion and rigorous discipline entailed certain inconveniences as far as the exploitation of their land was concerned. The monks had to rely on the soil—on unproductive and uncultivated lands—to make a living and to be able to discharge their obligations to guests and the poor. To meet these difficulties, they decided to admit lay brothers and paid workers. The brothers would be true religious, treated equally with the monks, but not strictly speaking monks, for the monastic state brought with it the obligation of living within the cloister and observing the Rule in its totality. Lay brothers were to reside in granges which would be set up in new clearings or near forests and they were to divide their days between prayer and work under the direction of the abbot, the cellerar, and a priest-monk who looked after their spiritual and temporal needs. With the help of the workers, they were to make their uncultivated abbey's lands productive and exploit them for the well being of their community.

Finally, the founders decided that they would found only abbeys, and not priories or cells. They took this step to conform to their new legislation and, above all the prescriptions of the Rule. Saint Benedict wanted the abbot present among his sons. He opposed monastic comings and goings, which the cluniac system had made necessary. To prevent abuses as well as forestall the danger of letting a temporary expedient become a definitive arrangement, they specified that no abbey was to be founded until an abbot and twelve monks were available; not least, they decided that their foundations were to be made exclusively in places removed from the noise of the world.

This is, in brief, what the founders of Cîteaux set out to accomplish. Although an apparently simple program, it had several unforeseen consequences. On the material level, the sober and mortified life of the poor, hard-working monks provoked ridicule among Benedictines in the neighborhood. The legatine imposition of peace and order notwithstanding, these former confrères resumed their harassment and calumny with vigor. Alberic was vigilant; he took immediate steps to free his monastery from vexation by securing the ideal canonical protection for it.

The Roman Privilege

After the death of Urban II, the office of permanent papal legate in Gaul passed from Hugh of Die to Cardinals John and Benedict. Alerted by rumors circulating about the New Monastery, perhaps at the abbot's request, the two dignitaries went to Cîteaux to inform themselves personally about the life of the monks. They advised the abbot and his brothers to seek Roman protection: by this they seconded the views of their predecessor and extended his protection over the monks. They left a letter of support addressed to the pope. Hugh of Die, the former legate and archbishop of Lyons, did the same in turn. Their own bishop, Walter of Chalon, was equally helpful. He drew up a petition requesting the confirmation of the measures taken at Port-d'Anselle establishing their independence from Molesme. Next he asked for the privilege called *libertas canonica*, autonomy guaranteed by the special protection of the Holy See, while respecting the rights of the local ordinary according to the law of the time.

> We humbly beg that you approve what has been done in accordance with our predecessor's order and the decision and rescript of the Archbishop of Lyons, then legate of the

Apostolic See, as well as of other bishops and abbots who
had been witnesses and participants in this decision . . . We
also beg you to deign to confirm by a privilege under your
authority that the place may remain a free abbey in perpetuity,
saving however the canonical reverence due our person and
that of our successors. [4]

Two monks, John and Hilbod, both natives of Arras, were deputed
to go to the Eternal City as delegates of the community. Bearing
the letters of the prelates mentioned above, they accomplished
their mission in worthy fashion. Paschal II granted their request
completely, according to a letter of the bishop of Chalon. The
liberty they had sought was given to them in the form of a valuable
privilege, the text of which implied their future exemption without
at that moment going that far: 'This abbey shall be particularly
sheltered under the protection of the Apostolic See, saving the
canonical reverence due to the diocese of Chalon'.[5]

Details of the Privilege

The text of the privilege made the exemption contingent upon
the conformity with and preservation of the newly introduced
observance. It would lose its validity if the monks returned to the
ordinary observance of the Rule. The pope entreated the monks
and all their associates to hold on to the newly inaugurated practices. He urged the monks to be mindful of their responsibilities
before God, who had by his Providence so manifestly led them.
Lastly, he threatened with ecclesiastical sanction and everlasting
punishment every ecclesiastical official and secular prince who
might be tempted to act rashly against the Privilege, while promising salvation and benediction to all who respected the peace and

4. *Exordium Parvum*, ch. 13; Van Damme, *Documenta*, p. 11. The petitions
of the cardinals and the archbishop form Chapters 11 and 12 of the *Exordium
Parvum*; *Documenta* pp. 10–11.

5. *Exordium Parvum*, ch. 13; Van Damme, *Documenta*, p. 12. Lekai, *The
Cistercians*, p. 457.

tranquility of the holy cenobites. The Roman Privilege was issued on 19 October 1100.

Exhorting the monks of Cîteaux to be fervent and to persevere, the roman pontiff divided them into two groups. The first was made up of new recruits, men who had recently renounced the 'broad roads of the world'. The second was composed of monks who had left a monastery (i.e, Molesme) where discipline had been less strict. It is surprising that those who had entered Cîteaux directly, without passing through Molesme, are mentioned before the 'old-timers' from Molesme. This seems to indicate that the younger members, those who had entered between 1098 and 1100, were as numerous as or even more numerous than, the founders who had returned with Robert to Molesme. If we estimate the number of veterans at half a dozen—the official account speaks of 'several'— then about fifteen pioneers had remained at Cîteaux. Those who had entered Cîteaux during Robert's administration or in the first months of Alberic's abbacy must therefore have numbered a good twenty. This would put the population at the time of the Roman Privilege at some thirty or forty persons. The attractiveness of the novelty, the favor of the duke, and Robert's prestige must have helped draw vocations to the 'wilderness' of Cîteaux.

The Roman Privilege and the reasons behind it—approval of the new observance at the recommendation of the diocesan and nearby bishops—had certain practical consequences which the bishop had already implicitly accepted. At issue was the normal expansion of the new abbey through the establishment of daughter-houses to which they wanted to hand on the same observance. For this they needed the approval of the ordinary. They faced an evolution which called for a new juridical constitution which would enable an effective supervision of the observance of the Rule and establish some sort of union among the abbeys. By giving his consent to the introduction of the new discipline, Walter of Chalon must have foreseen and accepted such a development in advance. This indicates that the bishop, working with Abbot Alberic, contributed to the creation of the new Order. By their example, vision, and unselfish zeal, Hugh of Lyon and Walter of Chalon contributed to the success of the reform.

White Cowl

Alberic is also credited with changing of the color of the cistercian cowl from black to white. To explain this change, admirers of the saint and of his work pointed to an apparition of the Blessed Virgin, who is said to have requested the white cowl as a sign of the special bond she wanted to establish with the Cistercians. Although greatly cherished by medieval authors and their readers, this explanation is nothing but a pious legend. The change was simply one of many consequences of the reformers' determination to follow the Rule and life of Saint Benedict in every detail. On the subject of clothing the Rule prescribes that the monks not be concerned about color. We naturally conclude that in full conformity with this advice, the monks decided to use darker wool, which soiled less, for work clothes and undyed material for tunics and cowls. The 'white' monks of Cîteaux were, incidentally, also called 'grey monks'—which suggests that the color they adopted was not bleached white.[6] This innovation was bound to raise complaints from the 'Black' Benedictines, even though white was already in use at other contemporary monasteries and had a long tradition in its favor.[7]

Material Possessions

Exceptionally well-endowed in intellectual and legal fields, Abbot Alberic was no less talented in matters economic. He managed to improve the financial status of his abbey, as circumstances necessitated, and to transform the institution of lay brothers, which had existed before Cîteaux, into an organization that supported the reform.

6. Othon Ducourneau, *Les origines cisterciennes* (LiguBé: Imprimerie E. Aubin et fils, 1933) 112–116.

7. Ursmer Berlière, 'La congrégation bénédictine de Chalais', *Revue Bénédictine* 31 (1914–1918) 402. Ducourneau, *Les origines*, 108–112.

During the first year of Alberic's abbacy, the Viscount of Beaune more than once came to the monastery to ask for the twenty *sou* which the duke had assigned him as the annual rent for having donated the land. When the abbot refused to pay, the sum remained in abeyance through the negligence of ducal officials. Informed of the matter, the duke took steps to ensure that the monks not suffer from such misunderstandings in future. He assigned to the viscount, several houses in the city of Beaune from which he was to receive the twenty *sou* directly each year. The case set an important precedent and proved a useful experience: in future donations of material goods the monks always tried, so far as possible, to add a clause that would keep them free from legal challenge. They aimed at a system of fiscal autonomy so as to be free from any payment and, consequently, from repeated transactions involving tithes, rents, and other dues. This precaution was intended, not to increase their possessions to the detriment of their ideal of poverty, but to safeguard the tranquillity necessary to the contemplative life. The primacy of the spiritual life is shaped by the spirit and practice of evangelical poverty, without which it cannot exist. This vigilance remained a tradition in the Cistercian Order. It may have inspired the first statute of its constitution, which prescribes that a mother-abbey can not exact any material contribution from her foundations.[8]

The second material advantage acquired through Alberic's shrewdness resembled the first, but constituted a real gain. The vineyard of Meursault, which the duke had donated in 1098, was still subject to an annual rent of ten *sou*, owed by the monks to a knight named Hugh of Chevigny. At the request of Duke Hugh II, who succeeded his father at his death on 7 May 1102, the knight agreed to receive this rent from the ducal officials. To his great credit, he even had it inserted into the deed that, should the ducal household fail to pay the rent, he would not reclaim it from the monks.[9]

8. Marilier, *Chartes*, nn. 22–23, pp. 49–51.
9. *Ibid.*, nn.12 and 25–26, pp. 12 and 57f.

We can also date two other land donations to Alberic's abbacy. The first was a tract of land at Gilly. It had been used by the monks of a local priory, a dependency of the parisian abbey of Saint-German-des-Pres. The principal donor of the land was Elizabeth, countess of Vergy. Aimo of Marigny renounced his seigneurial rights. The abbot of Saint-Germain, who signed in the name of the monks of Gilly, was named Raynald. There are no dates in the text of these acts, but the signatures allow us to assign them to Alberic's administration. Guy III, Count of Saulx, who signed as a witness for Haymo of Marigny, died in 1110 and could not have witnessed anything after that year; and Raynald, who served two abbatial terms at Saint-Germain, was not the abbot between 1108 and 1110. Correlation of this data allows us to date the acquisition to the time of Alberic's abbacy. This donation was later developed as the vineyard of Gilly, better known by its later name, the Clos-Vougeot.[10]

Around the same time Elizabeth of Vergy made still another donation, a large piece of land in the township of Gergeuil destined to become a grange. This was in fact the Cistercians' second grange, but the first erected by them, for on the now abandoned site of the original monastery there was already a grange called la Forgeotte (*Fabrica*).

Relocation of the Abbey

Little is known about the relocation of the monastery. The event is commemorated by a memorial stone marking the dedication of the church which the monks had built in place of the chapel which had been there when they arrived. The text of the inscription reads:

> This, the first church of Cîteaux, was built in 1106 and consecrated to the glory of God on 16 November [of that year] by the venerable Walter, bishop of Chalon, invoking the

10. *Ibid.*, nn. 33–35 and 41, pp. 57 and 63–65.

triumphant Queen of Heaven, the powerful Virgin Mother of God and ever-watchful Patroness of the Cistercians.[11]

Finding a new location had become necessary, not because the first site was overpopulated but probably because a major highway ran alongside the place they had hastily settled in 1098 and because they needed a better water supply. With no lack of worries in their undertaking, the monks certainly lacked resources. Only the love of poverty, which must be the normal climate of the monks' life, sustained their courageous zeal in trying circumstances. The project was completed.

Enduring Influence

Alberic contributed to the accomplishments of his successor and the whole future of the Order from an economic viewpoint and in every other way by admitting lay brothers and salaried workers, already something decreed by the whole group of founders. The brothers and workers assured the livelihood of the monks who lived inside the cloister and allowed them to devote their time to prayer, study, and work in the scriptorium, without doing too little or too much in the way of the manual labor prescribed by the Rule. Since two granges, not open to monks but entrusted to the brothers' care, were erected in Alberic's time, brothers clearly lived in them then. It is also undoubtedly due to the brothers, at least in part, that new buildings could be constructed.

For his labors on behalf of the temporal well being of his abbey Alberic fully deserves the praise we read in the *Chronicle of Mortemer*: 'Through the solicitude and industry of its new father [Alberic] and with God's generous assistance, the New Monastery advanced in holiness, excelled in fame and witnessed an increase of its temporal goods within a short period of time'.[12] This did not turn the founders from their ideal of poverty.

11. *Ibid.*, n. 27, p. 53.
12. *Auctarium Mortui Maris*; PL 160:392.

Social Significance

Alberic and his monks contributed in an appreciable way to the rise of a new social class: the free workers. The salaried workers admitted to Cîteaux, like most of the lay brothers, had been recruited from among their 'guests'. 'Guest' at the time meant primarily former serfs who had been freed from the service of a lay or ecclesiastical lord in return for their services, through the special favor of their masters, or by escaping into 'alien territory'. Having gained their liberty, these men had to look for a patron who would give them work; in the meantime they relied on public or private charity. Banding together, they formed groups constantly on the move between churches, abbeys and castles. Their freedom became complete only when they found permanent work, for this enabled them to think about establishing a home—usually in some hamlet in the shadow of a castle or an abbey. The explicit reference to the admission of salaried workers in the cistercian reform plan shows the christian solidarity which the White Monks felt with this class of poor men whose sparse and restricted life they had freely chosen to share. This solidarity provided effective aid to the formation of a new class of free men and led the monks to view things on a wider scale. Their part in seeing this class of free workers attain social emancipation was an effort worthy of the christian and monastic ideal.

The Monks' Sadness

It is customary to visualize the community as living and working according to the rhythm of the days and seasons, under the watchful eye of its abbot. The day of the church's dedication in 1106 was the high point of their extraordinary labors and, simultaneously, the beginning of a period of more stable and peaceful—that is, less intense—activities. The spirit of simplicity continued to inspire the monks and to shape their lives. The community blossomed and expanded to become a vigorous, joyful, happy family which radiated joy.

But a severe test was about to fall on the community. The austerities it had embraced with great fervor attracted curious and interested visitors, but because these practices differed greatly from the customs of other abbeys, they did not join as postulants. Those whom the Holy Spirit seemingly sent to share the ideals of these monks and to become 'heirs of their poverty',[13] only rarely moved from admiration to emulation, love, and commitment. They went away, perhaps sadly. Their departure saddened the monks. Alberic went to his grave with the heavy cross—humanly speaking—of seeing his little flock diminish to the point where he feared its extinction.

The monks' sadness reached low ebb on 26 January 1108, when their father left them to receive the reward of his struggles, labors, austerities, and prayers in heaven. The radiance, genius, courage, and patience of their leader filled them with admiration and gratitude. But these very qualities heightened apprehension over the succession as well as the sense of breakdown and sadness brought on by knowing themselves to be orphans.[14]

13. *Exordium Cistercii*, ch. 2; Van Damme, *Documenta*, p. 22.

14. Certain particulars of this biographical study have been explored in greater detail in my article, 'Vir Dei Albericus', *Analecta SOC* 20 (1964) 153–164.

saint
stephen
harding

STEPHEN HARDING

LBERIC'S ABBACY ENDED in an atmosphere heavy with sadness brought on by a lack of vocations. Stephen's abbacy began on the same sad note, but sighs soon gave way to songs of joy. A new springtime bursting with vitality was about to dawn. But before we continue our story, we must pick it up again at the beginning—where we sketched the historical setting of the monastic renewal. We must go back to the time when Saint Robert, a champion of renewal, made his first attempt at reform.

Stephen Harding, the successor of Robert and Alberic, was born in England around the year 1059. During his childhood and adolescence William the Conqueror invaded and transformed the country. The circumstances of the Conquest dislodged him to the Continent, where an important mission was waiting for him.

Stephen's father was a member of the Harding family, which belonged to the upper nobility. His name evokes the name Hading, the great-grandson of Dan, first king of Denmark and brother of Angul, the founder of Anglia (England). The people living in the regions of Jutland, Frisia, and the mouth of the Elbe, pursued by the Huns, migrated during the third and fourth centuries to the British Isles, where, one after another, they forced the Celts and Britons, the first known inhabitants of these areas, to retreat.[1]

1. *Saxonis Gesta Danorum,* Compendium liber I, in *Scriptores Minores Historiae Danicae Medii Aevi,* vol. 2, pp. 219ff. The difference of the consonant between

According to the Domesday Book of 1086, the Harding family held manses and tracts of land in Dorset, in the immediate vicinity of Sherborne, where Stephen once lived as a Benedictine. One of these tracts was located at Merriott, Stephen's probable birthplace. The same register also mentions that one branch of the Hardings was surnamed Fitz Elnod (*filius Elnodi*), while the other simply called itself Harding. An Elnod Harding was well-known for his high rank and exploits. A squire of King Harold, he left his post after the Battle of Hastings in which the king was killed. The remnants of the Anglo-Saxon army fled to Ireland and England came under Norman rule. Elnod became governor under William the Conqueror, while retaining his title of squire at the royal court. This Elnod was very probably the grandfather or great-uncle of Stephen Harding.[2]

As governor, Elnod had no better luck than he had had as a military commander. He faced a difficult task. First of all, he did not enjoy the favor of the people. But, it should be said in his defense, if Elnod had been disloyal to Harold's cause by joining the Normans, Harold himself had been unfaithful to William the Conqueror, whose rights to the crown of England he had previously acknowledged. People neither accepted the loyalty oath Harold had sworn to William nor acquiesced in the conquest of England. Instead of seeking to appease the rancorous and conciliate the dispirited, Elnod proved harsh. He dismissed the English, his compatriots, from every dignity and public office. According to the historian William of Malmesbury, he was intolerant, while his sovereign, although a foreigner, showed himself much more considerate toward the conquered people, at least at the beginning of the occupation.[3]

----

the two names of Hading and Harding can be explained by a frequent linguistic phenomenon found in the Danish language which, for instance, writes *Christiarnus* for *Christianus*. Since we are unable to elucidate this point, we leave it to the philologists.

2. We have treated this and other details of Stephen's life prior to his entrance at Molesme in an article, 'Saint Etienne mieux connu', in *Citeaux* 14 (1963) 307f.

3. William of Malmesbury, *De gestis regum Anglorum*, liber III. 254; PL 179:1236.

Post-Conquest Troubles

One of Harold's sons left his refuge in Ireland to incite an insurrection against the Conqueror among the inhabitants of Dorset and its neighbors. William sent an army under Elnods' command against them, but the former squire who had come to grief in the magistracy, now floundered in war. His army failed to ward off the enemy, and Elnod was killed. Harding Fitz Elnod's father became the object of scorn, as the pointed remark of his biographer attests: 'He was much better in quarreling than in the art of war'.[4] His successor as head of the army suppressed the revolt and expelled the surviving Anglo-Saxon troops.

As happens in such cases, the uprising had consequences all over the country and provoked reprisals. Villages were burned to the ground, prisoners of war killed, and citizens exiled or forced to flee, cut off from all contact with their families and deprived of all livelihood. The secret aid these unfortunate victims received came from relief activities centered around the abbeys and this led to the destruction of several monasteries and a massive deposition of abbots and bishops. Norman priests or monks were installed to replace Anglo-Saxon prelates and the abbeys were stripped of their goods and personnel.

Willingly or under constraint, Rome acquiesced in these radical changes. But the stance of the highest spiritual authority did not calm spirits or end suffering. The dioceses founded earlier by missionary monks had been attached to ancient abbeys. Most of the bishops were monks and all were natives of the country. The goods of the dioceses were not distinguished from the goods of the abbeys, which were more ancient and far better endowed than the bishoprics. When the episcopal sees were abruptly taken over by foreigners, the bonds with the past were ignored or broken. The norman bishops, following their whims or looking for personal profit, transferred their sees, to the utter consternation of both the faithful and the monks and to the detriment of the established ecclesiastical and economic order. Among others, the abbot-bishop

4. *Ibid.*

of Sherborne, a newly appointed norman churchman, transferred his see: Salisbury (in Wiltshire) became the episcopal see of Dorset. But the bishop remained abbot of Sherborne, and this double title was passed on to his successors until 1122. Any protest against these measures was severely punished. Those who had been personally victimized did not even have the right to complain. It was a crime to 'flee from the king's wrath', and one bishop, a former monk-bishop sent back to his monastery, was forced to declare that he had taken his decision voluntarily, because of his 'distaste for the noise of the world'.[5]

Monk of Sherborne

All this helps us understand why Stephen Harding, once a monk of Sherborne, left the monastery of his profession and his country to continue his education and life under the skies of France.

According to his biographer, Stephen received his first education in the schools of his homeland, probably at Merriott. While still a boy (*puer*), i.e., at about twelve and thus around 1071, he entered the benedictine abbey of Sherborne as a novice. This was exactly the period of post-invasion troubles in which the abbeys were involved, especially those in the Southwest and most specifically those that contained the family members of such 'partisans' as the Hardings, the relatives of Elnod.

During these trying times, Stephen must have had reason to fear for his life and deplore the lack of peace in the area. He left Sherborne to flee to Scotland, awaiting his chance to move on to France, where he wanted to continue his studies. Much later, at the end of his long life, he wrote a letter to his former confrères in which he mentioned that he had been one of them, the youngest among them and someone of no importance. He seemed to allude to the circumstances of his departure when he wrote that, while the Lord had been pleased to fill his empty heart with an abundance

5. Augustin Thierry, *Histoire de la Conquête d'Angeleterre par les Normands*, vol. 2 (Paris, 1825) 115–119; see also p. 211.

of graces, they—his former brothers—'had been far superior to him in their holy profession because, trusting in God, they had the strength to persevere in the religious state'.[6] This form of expression insinuates a difficulty that was shared by everyone, but to which people reacted in different ways. Stephen implicitly accused himself of having lacked confidence in God.

We must, therefore, conclude that when the young monk left Sherborne, he acted either out of prudence or out of fear and that he had no intention of taking back the religious habit in another abbey or in the monastery of his profession, if peace ever returned to it. Or should we, at this point, believe a contemporary who attributed his departure to a 'disgust for the monastic life and a longing for the world'?[7] We think that the charge of apostasy must be rejected, for the explanation of the english writer is wholly consonant with the literary style of the time and, despite the chauvinism that inspired him, he would have risked offending the sensibilities of his countrymen for a long time to come if he had expressed himself in too realistic a way. Although Stephen had the humility to admit his lack of trust, we know that he had special reasons to fear for his safety and that he did not wish to endanger his community.

Student in Exile

Once in France, the foremost center of learning in Europe, Stephen attended several cathedral schools—probably the school of Rheims and perhaps also those of Laon and Paris. This formation in ecclesiastical and secular learning may have gone on for ten years. During this period—which is relatively long to our way of thinking but quite normal for the age—the young man may have kept in contact with his family or else enjoyed the goodwill of a benefactor. It is also possible that he earned his own living through manual

6. The letter is printed in C. Hugh Talbot, 'An Unpublished Letter of St. Stephen Harding', *Collectanea OCR* 3 (1936) 68; and in *The New Monastery*, ed. E. R. Elder (Kalamazoo, 1998) 88–89.

7. William of Malmesbury; PL 179:1287.

work, writing, or manuscript illumination. His activities in later
years allow the conjecture, but we know nothing precise about this
period, until he met an English cleric named Peter.

A professional pilgrim who traveled to the most famous shrines
on the Continent, Peter visited abbeys, hermitages, and persons—
both priests and laymen—renowned for their holiness and teaching. One day, while making his way along near the border of
Champagne and Burgundy, he came upon his compatriot Stephen,
living alone and devoting himself with great fervor to prayer and
the christian virtues. Filled with admiration for his recollected and
mortified life, Peter asked and obtained Stephen's consent to live
with him and share his life. The two lived together for some time,
supporting each other in the pursuit of perfection. Every day they
recited the whole psalter together, alternating its verses.[8]

One day Stephen and Peter decided to make a pilgrimage to
the Eternal City, 'in order to pray there'. They began the journey
without abandoning their customary daily psalter and they stopped
along the way to visit shrines and saintly persons as they made their
way south. In the process they visited the monasteries of Saint
Romuald at Camaldoli and Saint John Gualbert at Vallombrosa.
On their way back from Rome, Divine Providence directed their
path to Molesme, which was by then a flourishing abbey. Both
decided to become monks under Abbot Robert. Since this abbey
was 'large' around 1085, it was probably then that Stephen and
Peter entered it.

Crisis of Conscience

The young monk, scarcely clothed in the monastic habit for the
second time, became acquainted with a benedictine life different
on several points from the practices he had learned and observed at
Sherborne. This is not surprising, for the english abbey followed
a tradition which differed from the customs observed by abbeys
which had been reformed and simplified in the ninth century by

---

8. *Vita beati Petri Juliacensis*; PL 185:1259.

Benedict of Aniane. In addition to 'official' differences, he must also have noticed others stemming from the crisis and transition Molesme was passing through.

His appraisal has been transmitted to us by William, a monk of the abbey of Malmesbury who wrote a biography of sorts around 1120. William offers certain details which hint that he had visited Cîteaux and talked with Abbot Stephen. He even records the arguments Stephen had proposed earlier at Molesme in an effort to promote the reform. Here, in brief, are the ideas he attributed to Stephen.

> The Creator of the universe has ordered all things according to laws, conceived and put into effect by divine wisdom. Human nature is subject to these laws, but its weakness often causes it to abandon the paths of wisdom which reason (*ratio*) points out. Inspired by God, Saint Benedict drew up a collection of laws to govern human life. Although he imposed some rules that do not seem reasonable, they must still be accepted on his authority. For authority and reason never contradict each other. No one may turn away from the Benedictine Rule without a justification drawn from the holy Fathers of the Church. Unless there are serious arguments against it, one must follow the Rule of Saint Benedict.[9]

We have already seen the practical consequences of these principles: the reform outlined in the previous chapter.

Ordericus Vitalis, another benedictine historian who wrote around 1135, records the arguments which the monks of Molesme used against each other. Unlike William of Malmesbury, he attributed the reform initiative to Abbot Robert. Robert presided at the discussions at which some of the brethren voiced objections to the proposed reform. Their argumentation ran like this: the example of the monks whom Saint Benedict himself sent to Gaul is to be preferred to the practices of the egyptian hermits. The

9. William of Malmesbury; PL 179:1288.

Rule allows great flexibility in food and clothing. Manual labor is the task of the peasants and salaried workers; the monks' job is to pray. On the subject of tithes—which, according to the future Cistercians, following the teachings of the Fathers, by right belong to diocesan clergy—Odericus noted that monks are in fact clergy.[10]

The two accounts are well founded and accord with the already-cited testimony of the *Exordium Cistercii*, according to which the monks at Molesme lived 'in a saintly manner' even though their life was not in full harmony with the Rule. Ordericus, after denouncing the literalism of the Cistercians, paid them a guarded compliment: 'Seeing their zeal and their austerity, I find nothing to reproach in them. But I do not think that they are better than our Fathers, who were truly great men and still enjoy universal approval'.[11]

Why did Stephen, the jurist, prefer the first opinion? The teaching of Lanfranc of Bec, which was considered authoritative and which Stephen and his brothers must have known, has left traces in the authentic account of the foundation of Cîteaux. Lanfranc taught that a monk could leave the place of his profession and change his stability for three causes: extreme poverty; excessive persecution; and irreligion within the community. These three reasons are derived from the purpose, or spirit, of the monastic vows, which is to assure one's salvation and give glory to God through the observance of the Rule. Whenever this goal is not attained, the famous monk-teacher recommended leaving the monastery and going to another place where it would be possible to achieve it. Otherwise one commits the crime of perjury: *ne perjurii crimen incurrerem*.[12]

The expression *perjurii crimen [scienter] incurrere* is found in the oldest manuscripts of the *Exordium Parvum* in reference to several monks at Molesme who, in their fear of perjury, decided to leave the

10. Ordericus Vitalis, *Historia Ecclesiastica*; PL 188:637–639.
11. *Ibid.*, PL 188:644.
12. *Judicium de stabilitate monachi in loco quem posuit*; PL 159:33–336. See also Charles Dereine, 'La fondation de Cîteaux d'apres l'*Exordium Cistercii* et l'*Exordium Parvum*', in *Cîteaux* 10 (1959) 128f.

monastery of their profession and look for another place where they could fulfill their vow to follow the Rule of Saint Benedict. This does not imply a condemnation of or contempt for those monks who continued to live 'in a saintly manner' at Molesme by following the almost universal observance of benedictine abbeys. But human weakness and the narrowmindedness of simple or superficial souls managed to open the door to petty quarrels.

Man of Learning and Man of Action

In attributing the initiative for reform to Stephen, the Cistercian Breviary repeats a very ancient tradition that goes back to William of Malmesbury. This is clearly confirmed by Stephen's canonical expertise, recognized from the Charter of Charity and his reputation as a canonist. His personality suited him to be his abbot's right-hand-man in dealings with the duke, the legate, the bishop of Chalon, and the ordinary of Vienne, the future Pope Callistus II. No one was better qualified to explain or to defend the reform cause or to bear the fatigue of traveling or to know court or chancery procedures than he, the former pilgrim, the scion of the highest nobility, the skilled scribe and expert in the formalities of the law.

Throughout his life, he had to undertake numerous journeys and negotiations: to collect or consult manuscripts of the Bible, the writings of the Fathers, liturgical texts or gregorian melodies and chants; to improve the financial state of his abbey and make new foundations; to obey the pope who charged him with a mission or invited him to ecclesiastical assemblies; finally, in times of disaster, to go begging to seek relief for the people living near his monastery.

It is no surprise to read in William of Malmesbury that he was elected abbot while away from his monastery. The description Stephen gives of his predecessor and of himself in this regard is very revealing. He says that Alberic loved 'the Rule and the brethren'. And that he himself loved 'the Rule and the place'. By expressing himself this way, he clearly describes Alberic as a constant presence at the house, always with his sons and watching over the implementation of the Rule, while he describes himself as someone accustomed to the road but faithful in his duties as a monk and homesick for the place where his sons were living—as was later to be the case with his son, Bernard.

A man of action, Stephen was no less a man of prayer—which is the chief duty of every monk. Legend says of him that whenever he entered the church he had the custom of closing the door-latch for a moment, reminding himself that he must banish every distraction that might arise from his numerous occupations and cares. Like Peter, his friend and former fellow-novice, he continued the daily recitation of the Psalter. Each recited one half. Peter continued this custom after returning to Molesme, following his participation in the foundation of Cîteaux. When Peter learned about Stephen's election, he took it upon himself to recite the whole Psalter every day in order to relieve his friend, for he knew that from then on he would be too burdened by his duties to do so.

The Scriptorum

The *Monitum* of the so-called 'Bible of Stephen Harding', written in 1109, tells us of the part Stephen had in this great enterprise. Did he remember that in his native country Archbishop Lanfranc had awakened the critical sense of the priests and monks by undertaking the correction of the Bible throughout the realm?

While copying the Bible, Stephen and his helpers, working under the direction of their abbot, noticed among the texts they used as models certain passages or readings which seemed suspect to them. The Book of Kings in particular had variants of a doubtful authenticity. They decided to examine the whole Bible by comparing different copies—collating them at Cîteaux or consulting them where they were. Their method improved as their work progressed. Stephen, who had in the meantime apparently become abbot, went to learned Jews to solicit their help. He described in detail how his request was received. The rabbis, speaking in the romanic tongue and opening their scrolls for him, showed him the respective passages in the original Hebrew and 'Chaldaic' languages. In this way Stephen personally convinced himself that the doubtful passages or verses did not figure in the authentic texts. He had the superfluous passages or verses erased in his manuscripts, as can still be seen in the volumes preserved in the Municipal Library of Dijon. The *Monitum* in question was meant to justify the corrections and to call them to the attention of any reader or scribe who might use this Bible.[13]

Among the chief products of the early scriptorium of Cîteaux we find Saint Gregory the Great's *Moralia in Job*. A brief note attached to the end of it gives the exact date of its completion: 23 December 1111. Somewhat later, the scribes of Cîteaux put the finishing touches to an 'ambrosian' hymnal, intended for the singing of the offices. Since Saint Benedict had mandated the hymns of Saint Ambrose, they had to go to Milan to locate authentic texts and melodies. Stephen took precautions against the inordinate zeal of innovators devoid of a critical sense by issuing a formal ordinance which future cistercian generations also observed: these hymns were never to be abandoned, for they were seen as forming an integral part of the Benedictine Rule and were therefore, in some way, included in the reform. The decree was drawn up in the name of the community, which at that time was the highest authority of the nascent order.[14]

Artist Monks

Experts have been effusive in their priase of the artistic qualities of the products of the scriptorium of Cîteaux. The initials constitute a priceless treasure among manuscript illumination, decorated as they are with foliage, interlaced branches, human figures, working monks and lay brothers, knights and biblical animals, with full-page miniatures representing Christ, King David, the prophets, evangelists, and biblical battle scenes. The colors have remained

13. Marilier, *Chartes*, n 32, p. 56.
14. *Ibid.*, nn. 38 and 31; pp. 59–55.

vibrant and the parchment is well-preserved, giving rise to the hope that these works of art will continue to bear witness in future centuries to the enlightened zeal and well-tried patience of the artist monks.

We must reject the idea that these beautifully illuminated texts were created by hired artists. The young foundation was too poor—as we have already seen and will discuss again later—to allow itself the luxury of entrusting to paid workers a job which the monks themselves were capable of doing, if need be without embellishment or color. In the extreme poverty of the early days they would most certainly have avoided paying salaries for the decoration of books destined for daily use. What is more, this miniature art did not enjoy the continued favor of their successors. In all probability, it was practised in the early days of Cîteaux only because of the personal talents of the founders.

Other clues, drawn from the style of the miniatures, reinforce the likelihood of this hypothesis. In these miniatures we discover the style of the 'Caroligian' tradition which was then in vogue in northern France. This is true, for instance, of the initial found at the beginning of the Book of Genesis and, in general, of every initial of the entire first volume; which is divided into two parts. The same style reappears toward the end of the fourth and final volume, at the point where the Letter to the Romans begins. This is quite easily explained if one admits that the group of scribes who used the carolingian style, having finished the first two volumes before the other group completed the last two, lent a hand to the others in order to bring the whole project to completion.

There were two monks at Cîteaux who had come from Arras: John and Hilbod. They had been chosen by Alberic to go to Rome to obtain the privilege which was granted in 1100. They must, therefore, have had a good intellectual and cultural formation. It was no doubt through their efforts, perhaps even their personal artistic contribution, that carolingian art, adapted to the Franco-Saxon genius, found its way into the cistercian scriptorium. To support this hypothesis one could additionally adduce the so-called

Psalter of Saint Robert, which the monks had brought along from Molesme at the time of their exodus in 1098. This book is done in the same style, and its first folios have a calendar which has several feasts of Saint Vaast (*Vedastus*) and a prayer of Bishop Fulbert of Chartres—all details which point to a northern provenance and indeed to a specific region and network of cities.

The third volume and most of the fourth betray an influence which is different from the one which characterizes the other parts of the Bible. Here the art work shows a striking resemblance to the embroideries of the famous Bayeux Tapestry. This tapestry recounts the story of King Harold and William the Conqueror from Harold's journey to Bayeux, where he swore he would recognize the norman duke's right to the crown of England, to his defeat at Hastings in 1066. It was woven and embroidered in England around 1070, a few years after the event. The figures of the soldiers as well as the shields and the colors in the two works of art are so similar that one cannot reasonably doubt that one influenced the other. The connecting link between the two is no doubt Stephen, on whose youthful imagination the arrival of invading armies in his country and his home must surely have made an impression. As a boy, he had learned to retell this story, to sing about William's triumphs and to sketch various scenes of the Conquest. As a young monk at Sherborne, he had the opportunity and the obligation of perfecting his writing and drawing skills. As a student and secretary, he had to practice with the pen and the brush. Finally, as a scholar, he retained an appreciation for beautiful and well-made books.

In spite of the contrast that exists, on one hand, between the art displayed in the manuscripts and the austere simplicity imposed by their poverty and, on the other, their pure and radical spirituality, the works produced in the scriptorium of the nascent abbey constitute a tribute worthy of the genius of the sacred texts and their authors. We need not wait for the invectives of a Saint Bernard against the frivolous sculptures and paintings of his day to appreciate the firm resolve of the Founders in aiming after a spiritual beauty which is characterized above all by the elimination of everything that might distract the monk from prayer.

Liturgical Simplicity

Until that time, the principle of authentic observances had never been applied in the area of liturgy. Stephen and his brethren decided to banish from the chapel, where they devoted the best hours of the day and night to prayer, everything that smacked of richness or superfluity. 'Franciscans' before Francis lent his name to it, they were lovers of Lady Povery, the mother and guardian of all virtues, and they demonstrated this in a more pronounced fashion than the Seraphic Father did himself.

They replaced gold and silver crucifixes with crosses made of painted wood, without the sculpted figure of the crucified Christ. They gave up liturgical vestments woven of silk and gold as well as all silver and gold trimming. They suppressed copes, dalmatics, and tunicles, keeping only chasubles made of fustian, albs and altar linens of unembellished linen, and woolen stoles and maniples. None of these vestments was to have silver or gilt embroidery. The chalices were to be of silver, gold-plated but not gold; the communion reed, for the reception of wine at communion, of silver. These precious metals were not allowed for any other liturgical function or, *a fortiori*, any profane use. The Cistercians were not the only ones to introduce such austerity into the monastic liturgy. They followed the solitaries of the Chartreuse and the cenobites of Afflighem. Later, in his *Apologia to Abbot William* Saint Bernard would become a zealous, even fiery, defender of the monastic ideal: the monk must live for God alone through the direct contact of love—without created images or material intermediaries.

Assuring Solitude

One other important measure marked the beginning of Stephen's abbacy. In accord with his brothers, he decided that thereafter neither the duke nor any other prince would be permitted to hold his court at the monastery, as they had been accustomed to doing on major feasts. For monks resolved to practice the benedictine ideal in its original purity, this custom of holding 'courts' at monasteries several times a year on the principal feast days constituted an abuse. The courts allowed the lords to attend religious services and take care of the tithes and rents which were due on these festivals. Even overlooking the nature of the business to be treated among the lords, the courts were hardly appropriate on religious solemnities. For two or three days the silence and peace of the cloister was disrupted by the din of neighing horses, rattling bells, clattering boots, clashing spurs, clanging swords, and the running-about of servants, with the monks busy caring for both men and mounts. Monks who had formerly been knights were able to recall memories of their own adventures and be exposed to the temptations this was apt to bring.

Anguish and Consolation

The foundation established by great toil faced another, increasingly alarming, problem: a crisis of vocations threatened its very existence. Already during Alberic's abbacy, the lack of postulants had become worrisome. Not only had an extraordinary mortality rate ravaged the community, but the harvests in Burgundy and surrounding regions had been poor; between 1109 and 1111 there was famine. The local plight and the general privation produced a double catastrophe and each made it impossible for the other to be remedied.

Deeply affected by the misery, Stephen decided to go begging to end the starvation of his sons. *The Legendary of Cîteaux* relates several miraculous events by which heaven stepped in on behalf of the hard-tried monks.

Another legend tells how God brought the vocation crisis to an end. Stephen, deprived of every human hope of the vocations which were essential to the infusion of new blood, abandoned himself to Providence. He reportedly charged a brother who lay on his deathbed to come back after he died and bring him a message from God, so he would know whether they should continue their life of austerity or not. The brother actually appeared, it is said, and reassured the abbot by predicting the entry of a large number of postulants. Whatever credence is given to this miraculous story, the solution to the problem arrived effectively in the person of a young knight named Bernard of Fontaines, the son of Tescelin the Red, and thirty relatives and friends—all seeking admission to the cistercian life.

New Donations

This abrupt enlargement of the monastic family created new problems. First, the community roughly doubled in size, probably, and this brought the need for new resources. But from then on they had the youthful manpower to increase their agricultural output. To obtain a reasonable yield proportionate to the available work force and their present and future needs, they realized that they needed to increase their arable lands. Even so, the primary concern of all the monks was to maintain poverty and their zeal for christian perfection. The *Exordium Parvum* recounts with eloquent simplicity: 'At this very time, the church [of Cîteaux] grew in lands, vineyards, fields and granges, but did not decrease in fervor'.[15]

As far as we can determine from the documents, the donations to which this text refers were Bretigny and Gemigny. The donor was once again Lady Elizabeth of Vergy, acting with the consent of her husband, Count Savary of Donzy. Among the other benefactors whose generosity made possible the erection of a grange on these properties, we read familiar names: Haymo of Marigny and the monks of Saint-Germain-des-Pres. The monks, unlike other donors who reserved no rights or compensations for their gift, obliged their brethren at Cîteaux to furnish each year six measures of grain—half in wheat and half in oats—to their steward at Gilly. Moreover, from the produce from the vineyards which they would

---

15. *Pain de Cîteaux*, n. 15, p. 146.

eventually plant on the land given to them, the Cistercians were to remit, again through the priory of Gilly as intermediary, a hogshead of wine for every twelve acres.[16]

Favorable Historical Circumstances

Once their numbers had increased, the monks had to think about founding new houses. A promising future loomed on the horizon. But before beginning this story, let us take a brief look at the political developments which framed the happy events they were about to experience. The text of the *Exordium Parvum* invites us to do so.

In Chapter X we read that the Roman Privilege had been obtained from Paschal II in the year 1100, 'before the same Pope Paschal had lapsed in the Emperor's [Henry V] captivity'. This is a clear allusion to the pontiff's capitulation when, deprived of his liberty and constrained by threats and humiliations, he granted the right of investiture to Henry V in the hope of avoiding even greater misfortunes for the Church.

At the time, the Investiture Controversy was passing through a turbulent phase, not only in Germany and Italy, but also in France and England. The extorted concession provoked a spirited reaction among all pro-gregorian ecclesiastics. In France, archbishops Jusserand of Lyon and Guy of Vienne, among others, wanted to summon a council to try the pope, but bishop Ivo of Chartres stopped this dangerous initiative and succeeded in eliciting a more conciliatory and filial attitude toward the incapacitated pontiff. As soon as he was set free, Paschal II hastened to calm the aroused spirits by informing Guy of Vienne of his firm intention to revoke the privilege. For this very purpose he convened a synod at the Lateran on 23 March 1112. The scandal was repaired and the freedom of the Church restored.

But Guy of Vienne, who had played an important role in this happy turn of events, was still not satisfied. He wanted to have every investiture conferred by a layman declared null and heretical and

16. Marilier, *Chartes*, nn. 39 to 39. IX. See also n. 51. pp. 59–63.

the emperor excommunicated. He even had his demands endorsed by a council which met at Vienne on 16 September that same year, but the pope, wanting to avoid the emperor's vengeance and wrath, considered it better not to go that far.

The attitude of the archbishop of Vienne holds great interest, for he had supported the reform from the beginning and had thus given proof of his enthusiasm for the Gregorian Reform which lay behind the monastic and canonical movements in general and the foundation of Cîteaux in particular. As was true of Hugh of Die, archbishop of Lyons and papal legate, Guy of Vienne took a personal interest in Cîteaux. Their solidarity with Cîteaux was reciprocal. A further proof of this lies in the conduct of Bernard and his companions, who entered this avant-guard abbey of the Gregorian Reform precisely at this critical juncture in the Investiture Conflict.

The entrance date of this large group of postulants is significant. According to the most probable calculations, they entered in April 1112, sometime before the twenty-first. This was just one month after the pontiff's release and the revocation of the extorted privilege. One can imagine the enthusiasm and renewed hope that seized every son and daughter of the Church devoted to the papal cause. The monastic world was greatly affected by these events. For Bernard and his companions, who some time earlier had retired to temporary quarters to prepare themselves for their entry into religion, it was the right moment to take the decisive step.

Guy of Vienne continued to lend his support in establishing the Order and, after becoming pope, he granted supreme confirmation to is—as the continuation of our story will show.

The Foundation of La Ferté

The collective entry of illustrious knights and clerics immediately changed the situation of the New Monastery and its prospects for the future. With the membership of the community suddenly doubled, the moment had clearly come to establish new monastic centers modeled on Cîteaux. The monks need to do more than simply increase their property holding and enlarge the monastic buildings—which could have exposed them to the danger of relapsing into the old ways they had set out to correct. In any case, their material crisis had just been remedied through the donations of Bretigny and Gemigny. They decided to seek lands suitable for the foundation of a new abbey.

Content but not unconcerned, Stephen began to negotiate with the lords of the area to secure the land he needed through their generosity. His intention soon became known to his bishop, Walter of Chalon, who always held him in great esteem and lively affection. The bishop contacted the counts of Chalon, lords Savary and William, who were quickly won over to the project and offered Stephen a property called Bragny, on the banks of the Grosne. Buildings were constructed on it with all the regular places—a chapel, chapter room, refectory, and the rest—so that the monks could live according to the Rule as soon as they arrived. Regular life began there on 17 May 1113. On the following day the modest chapel was consecrated by Bishops Walter of Chalon and Jusserand of Langres. The presence of the bishop of Langres showed that bonds of friendship between the monk-founders and the bishop of their 'mother', Molesme, endured. Neither Stephen nor Lady Elizabeth of Vergy, the great benefactress of Cîteaux, nor her husband and brother-in-law, both of whom were counts of Chalon and the temporal founders of the new abbey, could have been absent on this solemn occasion. The monk Philibert was made abbot and the foundation was named La Ferté, symbolizing the auspicious fruitfulness of the abbey of Cîteaux and the long line of foundations that were to follow.

The first foundation raised a serious problem: the juridical relationships, first, between a mother-abbey and daughter-house, and then between a mother-abbey and the local ordinaries. As we shall see, another major problem would also arise, but it was resolved by the Charter of Charity and the obstacle surmounted.

The First Charter of Charity

> As soon as the new plantation began to produce offshoots, blessed Father Stephen, in his watchful wisdom, provided a document of admirable discretion which served as a pruning knife to turn away the outgrowth of division which, if unchecked, could suffocate the fruit of mutual peace. Very appropriately, he wished the document to be called 'Charter of Charity'.

This testimony of the *Summa Exordii et Cartae Caritatis* agrees with the first lines of the Prologue of the Charter of Charity:

> Before the cistercian abbeys began to flourish, the lord abbot Stephen and his brethren, seeking to avoid a future shipwreck of their mutual concord, in this decree made clear, ordained and recorded for their successors, by what bond, in what way, and, most importantly, by what charity, although scattered in body throughout abbeys in diverse parts of the world, they should be indissolubly joined together in spirit.

The Charter of Charity, as it existed before the foundation of La Ferté, that is, in 1113, contained, in our opinion, the following wording:

> Since we realize that we are servants, albeit unprofitable ones, of the one true King, Our Lord and Master, we impose no exaction of any temporal possessions or earthly goods on our fellow-abbots and fellow-monks whom God's goodness, using us—the poorest of men—as his instruments, will place under the discipline of the Rule in various regions.
>
> For, wishing to be of service to them and to all the children of Holy Church, we make no provision that would burden them or diminish their temporal goods, lest while seeking to enrich ourselves from their poverty we should ourselves fail to escape the evil of avarice which, according to the Apostle, is the service of idols. We do wish, however, to retain the care of their souls for the sake of charity, so that if they should ever

attempt, even if only in a small way (*paululum*), to stray from their sacred resolve and the observance of the holy Rule— God forbid—they may through our solicitude be enabled to return to the right path of life.[17]

The Charter expressed the well thought out decision of Stephen and his brothers on two constitutional points: the renunciation of any monetary contribution or material payment by a daughter-abbey to its mother-house; and, yet an affirmation of their resolve to watch over the observance of the holy Rule in the new foundations 'for reason of charity'. While the founders were free to renounce the right to contributions which custom accorded them, they could not arrogate the right of imposing their vigilance in the matter of observances. This right belonged to the local bishop, who also had to give his consent before a foundation could be made in his diocese. Thus, if they wanted to make a foundation according to the provisions of the charter of Charity, they had to assure themselves of the prior agreement of the bishop.

These two statues presuppose a law enacted between 1098 and 1100, by which only abbeys were to be founded, in conformity with the spirit of the Rule and the example of Saint Benedict. But in 1100, and several times later on, the pope forbade the elevation of a cluniac cell or priory to the status of abbey. This was no doubt intended to stem the rush toward independence and remove the danger of relaxation. The prohibition also got around the delicate situation created by the Investiture Controversy, for every time an abbey was founded the problem of the abbot's investiture arose. The Cistercians had reasons to be happy that they had obtained the privilege as an independent abbey through papal confirmation 'before Pope Paschal lapsed'—a failing we know about.

The difficulty which had hindered the founding of abbeys disappeared after the revocations of lay investiture changed the political atmosphere, and the danger of relaxation had been removed by the

17. Van Damme, 'Autour des origines cisterciennes', *Collectanea* 20 (1958) 46–50.

Charter of Charity, the bishop's acceptance of which constituted a
'practical' delegation of his right of correction to the abbot-founder.
The Charter also brought into the relationship between the bishop
and the monks an element thitherto unknown, for it made the
abbeys' exemption from episcopal authority superfluous. For this
reason too, it deserved the name Charter of Charity.

Other Foundations

The thirty young men who entered Cîteaux in 1112 made profession in May or June 1113. After thirteen monks had left for
La Ferté, the population of the New Monastery was still dispro-
portionate to the size of the buildings and material resources. As
the newly professed moved from the novitiate into the community,
the need for another foundation became apparent. The hopes of
a priest named Ansius, living alone in the solitary place called
Pontigny, answered the monks' need: the devout hermit offered
them his property, on which there was a small church.

This time a new element, not present in the first foundation,
entered the picture: the foundation was to be made in a diocese
other than Auxerre, the home of Cîteaux. Walter of Chalon had
been so keen on the foundation at La Ferté that he was, in a
way, its co-founder. He was well-informed about the history of
the monks and their distinctive observances. The new legislation
formulated by Stephen and no doubt set down in writing was
known to him and had received his total and complete approval.
At the time of the second foundation, however, the monks need to
acquaint Bishop Humbald of Auxerre with the principles of their
reform. Accordingly, the only condition they set before accepting
the priest's offer was that the bishop should voice his consent.
Stephen, accompanied by Ansius, informed the bishop of their
common desire and asked for his approval. Humbald indicated his
willingness and quickly approved the juridical provisions of the
Charter of Charity and Unanimity.[18]

18. An expression used in the foundation charter of Pontigny, written after the
event. See Tiburtius Hümpfner, *Exordium Cistercii* (Vac, 1932) 19; and Marilier,
Chartes, n. 43, p. 66.

The property around the little church was inadequate to support a community, but Stephen easily obtained additional donations from the Count of Auxerre and other benefactors. On 31 May 1114, regular life began in the new abbey under the direction of Abbot Hugh of Vitry, a friend of and novice with Saint Bernard.

In 1115, two other foundations saw the light of day: Clairvaux, under Bernard; and Morimond under Arnold of Carinthia, another companion of Bernard both as a student at Rheims and a novice at Cîteaux.

More foundations followed in quick succession: at Preuilly, La Cour Dieu, and Bonnevaux. By 1119 Cîteaux could count seven direct foundations. One of them, Clairvaux, had in the meantime established Trois-Fontaines in the diocese of Chalons-sur-Marne. By the end of 1119, Cîteaux had twelve daughters and grand-daughters and by the end of 1123, twenty. This rapid expansion was checked only around 1150, when the Order numbered five hundred houses. By 1152 the monks realized that this rapid increase—which accelerated during the pontificate of Eugene III (1145–1153)— had to be halted. They hoped that this result could be obtained by prescribing a new procedure which assured a slower and more cautious expansion.

Toward a More Complete Charter

Between the unexpected success of the reform and the contents of the Charter of Charity of 1113 there is a connection. The Charter, as we have seen, made exemption from the local bishop's authority unnecessary; thus in an indirect way, it favored the Order's expansion but it also had the effect of guaranteeing that any lands to be donated would be cultivated by monks, lay brothers and hired workers, while any tithes or other revenues attached to churches and altars would remain with the diocesan clergy. All the material emoluments would remain with the local population and not, as was the case in the cluniac system, be moved to a central abbey in a foreign country. And the bishops' responsibility was lightened by the oversight the Father Abbot gave his foundation.

Even so, the original text was too concise and left several details unclear: these were left to the improvisation of the local superiors and bishops. In the early years they followed custom and custom became law. This law needed to be put in writing, once all the interested parties—abbots, bishops, and monks—had been heard. The Bull of 1119, which will be discussed later, mentions the part the monks played in elaborating the text that was approved that year.

Between 1113 and 1119, several events took place which help elucidate this historic development, that is, the cooperation of the bishops.

William of Champeaux, the bishop of Châlons-sur-Marne, had bestowed the abbatial blessing on young Bernard, abbot of Clairvaux, and he received, according to the norms of canon law and the Rule of Saint Benedict, Bernard's promise of fealty, saving the institutions of the new Order. Their first meeting began a lasting friendship between the two leaders. The bishop always exercised an enlightened protection over Clairvaux. His intervention already in 1116, one year after its foundation, had staved off a grave crisis which threatened to ruin the new abbey. The prelate went to the abbots' meeting for this very purpose, demonstrating by this step that he recognized the authority of their chapter. Somewhat belatedly, he requested from the same authority a ruling that Bernard moderate his zeal and be subject to his care in any way needed to restore his impaired health. Bernard agreed to retire for one year, from 1118 to the middle of 1119, to recover his strength. At the same time William consented to the establishment in his diocese of the abbey of Trois-Fontaines, a daughter-house of Clairvaux.

Guy of Burgundy, the archbishop of Vienne who had supported the foundation of Cîteaux, continued to show a lively interest in the Cistercians. In 1117, returning from a trip to Dijon, he visited Cîteaux and asked for some monks to found an abbey in his diocese. He used all his influence, his authority, and even his personal fortune, to procure property for the founders. The monks installed themselves at a place called Bonnevaux on 25 September 1118, but various difficulties, caused in part by the monks of Saint

Peter who opposed the foundation, delayed matters until 11 July 1119. Guy of Vienne, who on 2 February of that year became pope under the name Callistus II, restored peace between the two parties. One aspect of this incident may have inspired a new statute in the Charter of Charity: when Abbot John of Bonnevaux complained about his great poverty to the knights of the castle of Moras and the abbot of Ile-Barbe, both knights and abbot promptly came to his aid. Informed of this Pope Callistus II and Abbot Stephen of Cîteaux were quick to take action and obtained from the monks of Saint Peter the renunciation of the tithes to which they were entitled from the estate of Bonnevaux. The new Charter prescribed that an abbot whose house falls into extreme poverty must explain his situation to the annual chapter, and the abbeys are to come to his aid according to their individual resources.

The church leaders who had accepted foundations in their dioceses prior to 1119 were: the bishops of Chalon (Cîteaux and La Ferté), Auxerre (Pontigny, Bouras), Langres (Clairvaux, Morimond), Sens (Preuilly), Orléans (La Cour-Dieu), Vienne (Bonnevaux, Châlons-sur-Marne (Trois-Fontaines), Besançon (Bellevaux), and Autun (Fontenay).

Once negotiations and agreements with benefactors were concluded and permission had been obtained for the donation properties administered by the ordinary, the various arrangements involved in every foundation gave rise to the regulations that needed to be made to update the Order's legal system. The abbots and their communities, faced sometimes with situations for which the imprecisions of the 1113 Charter offered no solution, had to discuss things with their bishop and the abbot of Cîteaux. Stephen was in the best position to coordinate these elements, the person most capable of synthesising. The result, the new Charter, was presented by 'Stephen and his brethren' for the pope's approbation.

Approval of the Charter of Charity
Stephen took advantage of Callistus II's sojourn in France. He

personally went to Saulieu, where, on 23 December 1119, the pope granted him a bull, approving the new legislation of the Order.

This supreme approbation was given to a text which is no longer extant. In content it was similar to the text of the *Summa Cartae Caritatis* as found in Chapters III-XVI in the manuscript of the *Usus Cisterciensium Monachorum* of the Municipal Library of Trent, No.1711. Chapter I and II of the collection form an introduction to the juridical text and attest that the series of chapters which constitute it had been confirmed by an assembly of twenty abbots after they had been approved by papal authority. The original— much more extensive—text of the first two chapter is found in the *Exordium Cisterciensis Cenobii*, also called the *Exordium Parvum*.

Chapters II and IV of the collection, completed by Chapters IX and X, agree—apart from a very few insignificant differences— with the Charter of Charity discovered by Joseph Turk, who called it *Carta Caritatis 'Prior'*; it goes back, in essence, to 1119. The other chapters—Chapters VII, VIII and XI-XVI—have the same content as the *Instituta Generalis Capituli* found in the first edition of these *Instituta* in ms 31 of the University Library of Laibach (Ljubiana), with the exception of five statutes which are not in the *Summa* and must therefore be dated after 1119.[19] Thus the document of 1119, not counting certain variants and the general arrangement of the statutes, contained the complete text of the *Carta Caritatis Prior* and the first list of the *Instituta Generalis Capituli*.

The annual chapter which brought all the cistercian abbots and the community of Cîteaux together under the presidency of Stephen Harding took great care to adhere strictly to the pre-scriptions enacted between 1098–1100 and to the contents of the Charter of Charity then being developed. The first ten chapters of the *Instituta* in all manuscripts are characterized as having been taken from these primitive sources. These first ten chapters are

19. Van Damme, 'Genèse des *Instituta Generalis Capituli*', *Cîteaux* 12 (1961) 36–41. Here we content ourselves with a general comparison.

also found in the Trent collection, where they form, as it were, the framework of the series. The author clearly wanted to produce a systematic work and to indicate that the statutes that followed—dating back to 1119—were simply later developments of the first ten statutes and went back similarly to the prescriptions of 1098–1100 and the *Charter of Charity*.

This theory points to the object of the papal approbation as it was formulated in the bull: 'certain chapters relating to the observance of the Rule' means the *Instituta Monachorum de Molismo venientium;* 'and others which you have deemed necessary for your Order and abbey' is a reference to the statutes that make up the *Charter of Charity*, especially those that deal with the General Chapter, reserved exclusively to the abbey of Cîteaux. The bull returned briefly to the same subject in the next sentence: 'These chapters and the Constitution [of the Order]'. The decisions of General Chapter fall into one of these two categories; they are directly related to them in virtue of their content and had emanated from the organ explicitly approved, the General Chapter.

Contents of the Charter of Charity

The most important new statues of the 1119 Charter are: first, the stress laid on the obligation to follow the Rule according to the observances of the abbey of Cîteaux; secondly, the establishment of the General Chapter as the supreme authority within the Order.

Let us look at a general outline of this Charter, adding a brief commentary and listing all the changes it later underwent under the influence of Pope Eugene III, Saint Bernard, and abbots Goswin, Lambert, Fastradus, and Gilbert of Cîteaux.[20]

The Preface names the Charter's author: Stephen, assisted by his brothers, the monks of the abbey of Cîteaux. This introductory

20. These four abbots directed Cîteaux and presided at the annual chapters between 1151–1165. We have described the evolution of the Charter during this period at some length in the study, 'La constitution cistercienne de 1165', *Analecta SOC* 19 (1963) 51–1-4. Hereafter, we shall abbreviate *Carta Caritatis* as CC, *Carta Caritatis Prior* as CC-I, and *Carta Caritatis Posterior* as CC-II.

remark, in the light of Statute 2, must be taken as evidence that in 1119 legislative power rested with the community of Cîteaux, which formed some sort of oligarchy. Next follows the prescription about obtaining a bishop's approval of the Charter before founding an abbey in his diocese. The last part of the Prologue introduces the next two statutes, outlining their content in a clear and explicit manner.

Statutes 1 and 2.[21] A mother-abbey shall not exact any payment from her daughter, but assumes the love-inspired right and duty of watching over its observances and of correcting any deviation in timely fashion. About the importance and limits of the corrections to be made there have been, since the beginning, fluctuations in the texts. A manuscript of the *Summa Cartae Caritatis*, Saint-Geneviève ms 1207—probably the oldest, although incomplete, text—carries the most severe formulation in this respect: 'No one shall deviate from uniformity, not even by a needle point' (*vel in apice devietur*). On the other hand, Trent ms 1711 gives the variant: 'They shall observe [the Rule] in one and the same manner'. The *Carta Caritatis Prior* (CC-I) imposes a penance if a practice differed 'in the slightest' (*paululum*); by contrast, the *Carta Caritatis Posterior* (CC-II), which dates from 1152, omits this stricture and simply says: 'If someone should stray from the observance of the Rule . . . .'

Statute 3. Uniformity of usages, chant, and liturgical books with what was being observed at Cîteaux. This statute confirms and refines what came before: the only norm for interpreting the Rule is to be the practice followed at the abbey of Cîteaux. All official—liturgical and legislative—texts were to be identical with those used at Cîteaux. Uniformity is presented as a sign and means of unity in charity. Its practical advantage was that it allowed monks who visited other abbeys to follow the exercises of that community. Chapter IX and X of the *Capitula* of 1119 list the books which

---

21. CC was early divided into chapters. A more recent usage divides it into thirty statutes. Statutes 1 and 2 constitute the first chapter.

had to be strictly identical with those used at Cîteaux; to this list the *Instituta Generalis Capituli* add the *Liber Usuum* which, like the statute prescribing it, dates probably to 1125.

Statute 4. A prohibition of privileges contrary to their observances. This statute is not in the 1119 text, but dates probably to 1125 and was inserted into the official text of the Charter in 1152, at the latest.

Statute 5. Honors to be accorded a Father Abbot visiting one of his foundations. He shall preside over the community exercises, but make no decision about its members.

Statue 6. The power and authority of an abbot visitor. He has the right to correct anything he finds diverging from the Rule or the laws of the Order. He cannot take measures about the temporal goods of the monastery he is visiting against the wishes of the abbot and the community.

Statute 7. A regular visitation shall be held at least once a year. In 1152, the Charter authorized the Father Abbots to delegate another abbot to acquit them of this duty.

Statute 8. The annual visitation of Cîteaux shall be made by the four Proto-abbots of the Order. This statute came into existence only in 1163.

Statute 9. Marks of respect to be shown an abbot-son who is visiting his mother-house. This statute is completed by Chapter 34 of the *Instituta Generalis Capituli*, which requires an abbot-son to make an annual visit of homage to his Father Abbot.

Statute 10. The reception of abbots of a different filiation and rules of precedence. These abbots are to take precedence over the abbot-sons, who are regarded as religious of the mother-house whereas the former are guests who have, according to the Rule, a right to respect. Precedence among the visiting abbots is assigned according to the seniority of the abbeys.

Statute 11. Extension of the bonds existing, according to the *Charter*, between Cîteaux and her foundations to the other filiations, with the exception of the General Chapter which meets exclusively at the abbey of Cîteaux. According to the *Carta Caritatis*

Prior, full and total obedience was to be given to the conventual chapter of Cîteaux, headed by its abbot. This perfect obedience seems to have ceased to be obligatory at an early date and became a simple duty to conform to the decisions of the chapter. In the meantime supreme authority passed from the community of Cîteaux to the group of abbots assembled in chapter.

Statute 12. The obligation of attending the annual general chapter is imposed on all abbots. According to the 1119 Charter, the end of the novitiate and profession of one of his monks dispensed an abbot from attending annual chapter; the Charter of 1152 no longer allows this as a reason for staying away. Illness continued to be a valid excuse, and from 1152 on the abbots of distant monasteries were permitted to attend this assembly every two, three, or even more years. Both texts of the *Charter of Charity* make mention of a delegate in cases where the abbot was prevented from attending in person. In the beginning this representative had to be the prior. Any unauthorized absence was punished. A 'lesser fault' in the early years, this sanction later became a 'severe offense'. The change took place at an unknown date, certainly before the end of the twelfth century.

Statute 13. The subject matter of capitular deliberations. The assembled abbots had to provide for their own as well as their monks' salvation by examining observances which were open to improvement by mending and strengthening the bond of peace and charity among all of them. This dynamic program opposed a rigid conservatism while it also checked any unhealthy impulse for change.

Statute 14. The abbots proclaimed each other in the chapter if any of them was known to be negligent in the observance of the Rule, too devoted to temporal affairs, or guilty of any fault at all.

Statute 15. The Charter of 1152 introduced a special procedure for dealing with conflicts between abbots and other serious cases. This innovation probably dates from 1125. Disputes between abbots or other grave offenses brought before the chapter were to be adjudicated by the chapter as the highest authority and no appeal was allowed. The chapter was empowered to suspend an abbot from his functions and even to depose him—a power which, according to Statute 24, normally belonged to the Father Abbot.

Statute 16. Any disagreement between abbots assembled in chapter was to be settled by a commission appointed for this purpose by the abbot of Cîteaux, whose decision could not be appealed. The first formulation of this statute, preserved in Chapter 31 of the *Instituta Generalis Capituli*, fixed at four the number of abbots making up this commission. The Charter of 1152 no longer speaks of a specific number. These commissions mark the beginning of the *Definitorium.* Its membership was apparently the same for a long time, for in 1147 the abbot of Savigny was permanently added to this body, which at the time consisted of the four proto-abbots.

Statute 17. The need for an evangelical solidarity among the abbots. If an abbey suffered from oppressive poverty, its abbot had to notify his confrères at Cîteaux and they were to hurry to his aid, each in the measure of his ability.

Statute 18. A 'widowed' abbey was protected by its Father Abbot. This provision, unknown at the beginning, appeared in the Charter in 1165. The election of a successor was to take place under the presidency of the Father Abbot. This is one point at which the Rule and monastic legislation was modified by the Cistercians, for traditionally the bishop had been designated to preside over these elections. According to the Charter of 1165, abbot-sons had a right to vote in the election of their Father Abbot. At about the same time, the Father Abbot received the authority to confirm the newly-elected abbot. This statute was especially important in the Cistercians' dealings with the diocesan bishop and had to be specifically approved by him at the time the foundation was made.

Statute 19. During a vacancy of the abbatial see of Cîteaux, the house was to be administered at first by the senior of its abbot-sons, the abbot of La Ferté. After 1165, the four proto-abbots were charged with this responsibility.

Statute 20. The abbey of Cîteaux was given a special statute to regulate the election of its abbot. First, a certain number of abbots, chosen preferably from among the abbots of her immediate filiation, were to be summoned and then wait fifteen days from the death of the abbot. In the beginning, these abbots were invited only to approve the choice of candidates: later they also had the right to vote.

Statue 21. Every monk of the Order was eligible for abbatial office in any cistercian abbey, according to the 1119 Charter. In 1152, passive voting rights were given only to the monks of the respective abbey and its filiations and then, if none of them was suitable, to its abbot-sons.

Statute 22. Prohibition against selecting an abbot from outside the Cistercian Order or providing an abbot to outsiders.

Statute 23. From 1152 onwards, an abbot could obtain release from his office by requesting it from his Father Abbot. The latter had to seek the advice of a regional council of abbots before granting it.

Statute 24. An unworthy abbot, that is, an abbot who was seriously negligent about the Rule or the laws of the Order but unwilling to give up his office 'spontaneously', could be deposed after four warnings from his Father Abbot and a council of the abbots of the area. At the beginning, they had to go to the local bishop and his chapter in such cases; the abbots could act only if the diocesan authority refused to step in.

Statute 25. If a community and possibly its abbot resisted the latter's deposition, the Father Immediate and his co-abbots who had pronounced the deposition were empowered to pronounce excommunication and punish them.

Statute 26. Brothers who, as a result of the preceding Statute, were banished from their communities but had come to their senses, were to be readmitted, like the prodigal son, into the abbey of their profession.

Statute 27. Except in the cases of revolt treated in Statutes 25 and 26, the right to dismiss or to readmit a monk belonged exclusively to his own abbot or to the abbot of the place to which he had been sent.

Statute 28. As a parallel to the case envisioned by Statute 24, the abbot of Cîteaux could be deposed if he deserved it. In the early days, the council of the three proto-abbots had to give him the four warnings mandated by the Rule and, if he persisted in his blameworthy conduct, denounce him to the diocesan bishop. If the bishop chose not to get involved in the matter, it became necessary to assemble all the abbot-sons of Cîteaux to pronounce deposition and proceed to a new election.

After 1152, the four proto-abbots gave the required warnings, but the decision itself was reserved to the General Chapter, with no recourse to the ordinary. If the matter was such that it could not wait until Chapter met, the decision rested with the abbot-sons and certain other abbots. The abbots assembled for this purpose and the monks of Cîteaux then elected a new abbot.

Statute 29. The sanction imposed by Statute 25 was also applicable to the abbot and monks of Cîteaux, in cases of rebellion.

Statute 30. The indulgence foreseen by Statute 26 was to be accorded as well to rebellious monks of Cîteaux, provided they regretted their misdeed.

Days of Happiness

Life went on in the Order. In the monasteries utmost care was given to liturgical prayer, the chief occupation of the monk. During the 'intervals', idleness was to be avoided and good use made of the monks' time through manual labor, intellectual work, spiritual reading, meditation, and personal prayer, as prescribed by the Rule. This is the steady uninterrupted rhythm of a benedictine monk's life. The offices, excessively long at Cluny, had been reduced to the dimensions assigned to them by the Rule, with the exception of the *Office of the Dead*, which was added to the canonical office at an early date to commemorate deceased relatives and benefactors.

After the hard work he devoted to the preparation of the *Charter of Charity* and the approval of the Order through papal bull, we should like to visualize Stephen, the father of all the Cistercians, living among his sons, speaking to them in conventual chapter, listening to their confidences, lavishing on them his counsel and encouragements, and visiting them in their work places, especially the workshop of the scriptorium. Nor would he have forgotten the lay brothers living on the granges; he watched over their spiritual progress and waited for the right moment to give them suitable statutes.

In obedience to the Rule and a statute of the *Charter of Charity*, he also had to welcome guests. A famous visitor came to him around the year 1120: the monk-historian William of Malmesbury. The picture of Stephen drawn by this learned compatriot shows every sign of a personal encounter. In it Stephen is described as pleasant in speech, agreeable to behold, and radiant with supernatural joy. These qualities endeared him to everyone. And, William added, God used this beloved servant to convey his love to all men. Blessed, therefore, is someone who hands his wealth over to God and uses the abbot as his intermediary! Stephen received numerous gifts; he kept only a few of them for the upkeep of his house and used the rest for the relief of the poor and the construction of his monasteries. Stephen's bag was a public cash-box for all who were in need.[22]

The monks' prayers and sacrifices drew valuable encouragement from the friendship shown them by Pope Callistus II. How great must have been their joy when they learned that the long and difficult negotiations with the emperor and the imperial bishops had finally been resolved by the Concordat of Worms. The Concordat, concluded in 1122, was the official end of a long bitter struggle, but the real end—complete success and a definitive victory for the rights of the Church—was still a long way off. When the pope died on 23 December 1124, he bequeathed his heart to the monks

22. William of Malmesbury; PL 179:1290.

of Cîteaux, who preserved it in a reliquary placed behind the main altar of their church. This relic, a symbol of the enduring friendship of the great pope of reconciliation, was to assure his lasting presence among the monks. It also reminded the abbots who met there every year of their solidarity with the pope and of their duty to work for the unity of the Church. Their prayers and activities in various parts of Europe powerfully contributed to the achievement and preservation of this unity.

Saint Bernard Enters the Scene

After the initial hardships of his foundation, the abbot of Clairvaux clearly came to life, matured by suffering and experiences which greatly enriched his natural gifts. Before he took on a role in the life of the Church at large, he appeared on the more modest stage of the history of his Order, which was about to go through a trying period. While its existence was in no real danger, it needed a new impulse in the areas of morale and legislation.

The first blow it sustained came from the cluniac monks. The roots of this conflict lay in the distant past, reaching back to the uproar that surrounded the foundation of Cîteaux in the years of 1098–1100. They cropped up again at the beginning of Pons of Melgueil's abbacy at Cluny and remained unresolved for many years. Pons succeeded the saintly abbot Hugh, whose abbacy had been long and prosperous, but the spiritual and administrative legacy he bequeathed to Pons was burdened by certain abuses which he had simply tolerated. Restrictions imposed by the new abbot checked certain extravagance in clothing and an overly great liberty accorded the monks charged with the temporal affairs of the abbey who, because of their office, frequently had to be on the road. These seemed to the monks in question to be inspired by a desire for 'innovations', which they once again began to decry in the conduct of the White Monks. These measures were similar to an early statute in the Cistercians legislation by which the Cistercians would found no priories but only abbeys in order to safeguard enclosure and the spirit of recollection, and other cistercian statutes which prescribed total conformity to the demands of the Rule in matters relating to food and clothing. The misfortunes which had fallen just then on the abbey of Cîteaux did not recommend the rigor of this observance. Pons was forced by his monks to give up his modest attempt at reform, leaving behind the impression of premature and imprudent zeal.

Instead of winning the monks over to his views, Pons let himself be led by them into broad paths. He went so far as to allow himself to make excessive expenditures and to lead a worldly life, while remaining obdurate and tight-fisted in conflicts over temporal matters. His conduct roused criticism from his old friends outside the abbey and revived opposition latent among his monks. His nomination to a cardinalate by Callistus II did not soothe spirits, but provided a pretext for him to increase his spending and harden his uncompromising character. The pope did not believe in the accusations levelled against the abbot-cardinal until Pons departed for the Holy Land without his permission. This mis-step earned him the disfavor of Callistus II, who judged it opportune to proceed to a new abbatial election at Cluny. Hugh of Marcigny was elected, but he died after a few months. Peter, called 'the Venerable', was chosen to succeed him in 1122.

Peter apparently fell victim briefly to the same exaggerated zeal that had marked the beginning of Pons' abbacy and that of Saint Bernard, his senior in abbatial dignity by seven years. The young abbot of Cluny found himself in a very difficult situation. The spiritual unrest in his community did not favor the necessary reform. Past practices had produced prejudices. On the other hand, the monks of Cîteaux had attained great success through the rapid multiplication of their foundations and the papal confirmation of their constitutions. In the bull of 23 December 1119, the pope even omitted the name 'New Monastery', which the Cluniacs had used to ridicule the Cistercians. Several White Monks were overly elated at these successes and by their provocative behavior rekindled old controversies. Their example lost all its force as a consequence and bred dislike rather than admiration among the simpler souls in the cluniac camp. Even the finest and most prudent Cistercians were convinced that their way of life was holier than the life of the monks belonging to the old benedictine tree whose peaceful possession of monastic values earned them a reputation for great fervor and produced genuine saints, both monks and abbots.

Something better is sometimes the enemy of what is good. Peter the Venerable collided with the cistercian 'better'. He had to be in solidarity with his monks, if he wanted to gain their cooperation for the common good of the monastery. Feeling he must state his views in this conflict, he sent off an open letter against the Cistercians in which he yielded, to some extent, to his emotions. With biting criticism, he answered charges the Cistercians had been circulating. He accused them of hypocrisy and reproached them for stopping at the letter of the Rule while forgetting its spirit, which should have kept them from violating charity. Responding to the charge of independence which the new monks had raised over Cluniacs' exemption from episcopal oversight, Peter extolled the total dependence of his monasteries on the bishop of Rome. In an ironic tone, he chastised their pretentious singularity and countered their charges with his love for the traditions and principles of genuine religious life. To a rigid uniformity of law, he preferred a healthy adaptation; to formalism, the charity that must inspire every religious practice; and to manual labor, the more noble work of the spirit.[23]

Bernard took this criticism personally, realizing that he had originally thrown down the gauntlet with a letter to his cousin Robert, who had left Clairvaux to become a Benedictine at Cluny. The young monk had been influenced by cluniac advisers who appealed to his conscience by reminding him of a promise which his parents had made in his name by offering him as a child oblate to God in the church of Cluny. They also sought to frighten him by talking about Bernard's severity, which they called inhuman. In

23. PL 188:166.

response, the abbot of Clairvaux sent a letter to Robert at Cluny,
pointing out to him that the cistercian life was more meritorious
than the cluniac, denouncing the abuses of the Black Monks and
reminding his young cousin of his responsibility before God.[24]
Several years later, after Peter of Montboissier, whom posterity
would call 'Peter the Venerable', had become abbot of Cluny, he
answered with the open letter we mentioned above.

Bernard may have preferred to let matters rest where they
were, but his friend, Abbot William of Saint-Thierry, insisted
that he reply. At issue was no longer one person's salvation, but
the reputation of his Order and the conscience of all his monks.
Accordingly, Bernard wrote his *Apologia ad Guillelmum*.[25] This
work, sometimes harsh and sometimes conciliatory, begins with the
admission that the author hesitates to write for fear of increasing
scandal rather than removing it. But he composed himself and
with an eloquent and charming argument professed his affection
for the monks of Cluny and his esteem for the good they were
doing in the Church. He explains the need for a variety of religious
orders, emphasizing that this variety must not violate the demands
of charity. In his heart he could wish to belong to all religious
families: by his profession he is bound only to one. He censured
those who scorned the monks of another observance, especially
those who rashly judged the conduct of the Cluniacs. Next he
discussed the superiority of spiritual labor over physical. Thus, in
the first part he condemned those of his brethren who belittled the
practices of the black Benedictines. But in the second part he laid
into the vices which the Cluniacs called virtues—and with what
force! He denounced their deviations from the Rule and from the
abiding principles of christian asceticism in the area of food and
clothing. He reproached the extravagant trappings of their abbots,
the opulence of their buildings, and the rich decorations which
desecrated the chapels of their houses. Explaining his attitude in

24. PL 182:67f.
25. For more on this subject, see *Pain de Citeaux*, n. 1, pp. 28–29.

the affair of his cousin Robert, he limited himself to expressing disapproval of those who turned fugitive through inconstancy. It was blunt and graphic language, but it never fails to safeguard charity or to point out the means of putting it into practice.[26]

This aside on Saint Bernard illustrates first, the atmosphere in which Stephen Harding was living and, secondly, the unity of heart and spirit between abbots, father and son. For, contrary to what is sometimes thought, the two abbots did not differ in their understanding of the sobriety and simplicity characteristic of the cistercian reform. Everything Bernard said in his *Apologia* is found in juridical form in the legislative texts which had been in force since 1119, and indeed since the very foundation of Cîteaux. Bernard held the man he called 'the Lord of Cîteaux' (*dominus Cistercii*) in great esteem and deep veneration. These sentiments were reciprocated by the Lord of Cîteaux, who liked to acknowledge and encourage the manifold talents of his son. We may mention in passing that in 1123, Stephen, accompanied by Bernard, attended the 'consecration' of the virgin Aremberga, daughter of Duke Hugh II of Burgundy.[27]

Times of Trial

The years of 1124–1125 were turbulent. After the pain and humiliation of a serious crisis, the Order emerged with a new vitality, as if its forces had been renewed. Its leaders were able to benefit from the experience of adversity and their Institute was firmly established on a foundation of law.

In the year 1124 a great famine ravaged the area. Long, harsh winters and summers without harvests depleted food stores.[28] Lords, bishops, and abbots all realized that they must offer help to

26. PL 182:895f.

27. Ernest Peit, *Histoire des ducs de Bourgogne de la race capétienne* (Dijon: Picard, 1885) 1:335.

28. Leopold Grill, 'Morimond, soeur jumelle de Clairvaux', in *Bernard de Clairvaux* (Paris-Aiguebelle: Edition Alsatia, 1953) 125f.

the populace. Bands of starving poor arriving from other hard-hit or less organized regions joined the local crowds, begging for a bowl of soup or a piece of bread. Clairvaux fed two thousand persons a day. The other abbeys did whatever they could in obedience to the Rule, which prescribes helping the poor and receiving guests. The abbot of Cîteaux organized a similar relief effort and, no doubt remembering what Saint Robert had done in 1095, went to Flanders to seek help for the burgundian population.[29]

Did Stephen meet the Count of Flanders, Charles the Good, like himself a descendant of a noble danish family, on this trip? Charles, the son of the martyr-king Knut IV and Adele, who later married Duke Roger of Apulia, had been on crusade twice and had succeeded Baldwin VII as count of Flanders and vassal of King Louis VI 'the Fat'. Deeply devoted to his people and unshakably upright, Charles made it his duty to distribute provisions stored up in the granaries of his country. But the following year the scourge also reached Flanders. He issued ordinances to assure the widest possible provisioning. Among other decisions, he prohibited beer–seeking to prevent the diversion of the grain supply. He imposed the growing of wheat and opposed usury. One family of unfree serfs particularly affected by his measures had to give up an enormous quantity of grain which was requisitioned for the common good. In an act of revenge, Charles the Good, who had no other intention than to relieve misery, was assassinated while at prayer in the church of Saint Donatian at Bruges.[30]

Even if Stephen did not meet the beneficent duke personally, he surely benefited from his wise administration. This journey to Flanders was probably the one that took Stephen to the abbey of Saint Vaast outside Arras. There he left a precious gift, a manuscript copied by the monk Osbert, a calligrapher and miniature painter. In one of the full-page miniatures, the artist depicted

29. *Ibid.*
30. Edouard de Moréau, *Histoire de l'Église en Belgique* (Brussels, 1945) vol. 3:13ff. ch. 1: " 'Le martyr", Charles-le-Bon'.

the abbots of Cîteaux and Saint Vaast flanking the Virgin Mary. Stephen is offering her his church.

The Morimond Crisis

Another abbot who fell victim to the disaster was Arnold of Morimond. He lacked both material resources, and the talent to procure them as well as the gift to assuage the spirits of those whose hunger he was unable to alleviate. We have already seen in passing that Morimond had been founded without adequate material resources. Yet, in spite of its great poverty, the abbey had already sent out three foundations: Bellevaux in 1119, La Crête in 1121, and Altenkamp in 1123. Arnold also cherished the hope of making a foundation in Palestine and had already designated the founders. When his monk Adam, the prospective superior, went to Clairvaux to seek counsel, Bernard remonstrated against the enterprise. Precarious conditions at home worsened on account of the famine. The privations forced on the community and the charge by its neighbors that Morimond did not follow the good example of other abbeys provoked discontent in the community. In the granges the lay brothers refused to work. Disorder increased from day to day, keeping pace with growing indigence.

Arnold decided to leave for the Holy Land with the designated founders nevertheless. It was flight. The plan might have seemed heroic under normal circumstances, though even then it would have to be regarded as foolhardy and untenable. Not only did they face the hardships of the climate and incessant wars with the Turks and the Muslims, but the laws of the Order prescribed annual visitations and a General Chapter of all abbots. The abbot of Morimond listened only to his own ideas and sought neither the advice nor the permission of the abbot of Cîteaux, his immediate superior. Armed with a papal permission obtained without the knowledge of his superiors in the Order, he restricted himself to informing the abbot of Cîteaux of his departure, adding in his message that it would be useless to call him back.

Arnold and his companions were staying at the time with the monks' families in Lorraine and the regions of Liége and Brabant. They knew that Stephen Harding had gone to Flanders and sent their messenger to meet him at Clairvaux. Since Stephen had not yet arrived, Bernard took the matter in hand.

He wrote several letters to various persons, hoping to steer the group of monks, in his opinion on the road to perdition, back to their senses and into their abbey. To his urgent pleas he added reproaches designed to prick Arnold's conscience: what right had he to leave his post under such tragic circumstances, disregarding the fate of his monks—both those who remained and those who departed—and refusing to recognize his lawful superiors, that is, his bishop, and his Father Abbot? Arnold had seized on the political device of a *fait accompli*, Bernard charged; he had used deception and run away from difficulties and humiliations on the hypocritical pretext of espousing an heroic cause! He disregarded the unanimous decision of the college of abbots and abandoned his responsibilities by his own will.

The adventure came to an abrupt end with Arnold's unexpected death in the early days of 1125. Because his sons were still scattered, an extraordinary General Chapter was urgently summoned.[31]

The history of this affair revealed the inability of the Order's government to prevent such machinations and misfortunes. The statutes approved in 1119 were too imprecise to restrain anyone from disregarding them, either in good faith or by a tolerably defensible subterfuge. Several points needed to be better defined; among them imposing on abbots a responsibility to submit their plans for a foundation to the approval of two co-abbots and a prohibition, under pain of nullity, against having recourse to any authority higher than the General Chapter. These new statutes, introduced in the form of capitular decisions and added to the

31. We have presented an outline of these facts, with detailed references, in the article, 'Genèse des *Instituta Generalis Capituli*', in *Cîteaux*, 12 (1961) 43–46.

Instituta Generalis Capituli, passed around 1152 into the revised *Charter of Charity*.[32]

An Important Change

This constitutional chapter, made necessary by the imprudence of one abbot, was not the only attempt at improving the Order's legislation. Plans for a *Liber Usuum* were also one of Stephen's concerns and hopes. But before we continue to describe the life and work of Stephen, we must take a brief look at a collection already mentioned earlier: the codification called *Summa Exordii et Cartae Caritatis*. An obvious similarity between the ideas of its author and those of Saint Bernard, and above all the provenance of the manuscripts, provide clues which tend to place its author in Bernard's immediate circle. [33] The author has a very personal style and reveals the talents of a gifted jurist. The work may be dated with great probability to the years 1123–1124, for prior to this time Cîteaux did not have the twenty abbeys mentioned twice in the text. Nor could it be dated to 1125 or later, for if it could, it would have to mention, if not the facts about Morimond, then at least the juridical consequences. But in this codification there is no allusion or even hint which would allow us to connect it with the extraordinary chapter held at the beginning of 1125.

The collection is an unofficial codification of the statutes as they existed in 1119. Its historical introduction informs us about an event of great legal importance: the twenty abbots assembled in chapter confirmed, either by their signatures or by affixing their seals, the legislation that had been approved in 1119. This capitular act must be seen as introducing a new structure into the government

---

32. Van Damme, 'Genèse', pp. 42–43.

33. Leopold Grill, 'Der hl. Bernhard als bisher unbekannter Verfasser des *Exordium Cistercii* und der *Summa Cartae Caritatis*', in *Cistercienser-Chronik* 66 (1959) 43–57. Grill's thesis is partially confirmed by Jean Leclercq, '*L'Exordium Cistercii* et la *Summa Cartae Caritatis* sont-ils de S. Bernard', *Revue Bénédictine* 73 (1963) 88–99.

of the Order. We know that the *Charter of Charity* and the other statutes had been submitted by Stephen and his sons, the monks of Cîteaux, for papal confirmation. Their conventual chapter was the core of their government and chief seat of authority. Through the force of events, this power was to pass from the conventual chapter to the chapter of abbots sitting with the community. The subjects submitted to chapter for discussion had a greater interest for the abbots than for the monks who, in any case, neither could nor should have been informed about everything that concerned the life of every single abbey. Four or five years later, by confirming the statutes of 1119 which had already received papal approval, the abbots endorsed the same set of statutes even though they had formally emanated from the community of Cîteaux. In this way they declared themselves the supreme authority within the Order, though without excluding from this authority the monks of Cîteaux, as participants. By acting in this manner, the abbots, the sole heads of their abbeys by general monastic law, transferred part of their authority to the college of abbots, recognizing the authority of the chapter which they had themselves helped to establish and to which at the same time they now subordinated themselves. This text seems to have been, and to have been intended to be, corrective to the text drawn up by Stephen in 1119. For all practical purposes, the monks of Cîteaux were excluded from capitular power. Some ten years later, the abbots would approve a simple rule that the monks of the mother-abbey of the Order must leave the chapter room before the sessions of General Chapters began.[34]

The *Summa Exordii et Cartae Caritatis* seems to have been drawn up for the benefit of novices. In a concise running narrative, it covers the contents of the *Exordium Parvum*, the *Charter* of 1119, and a systematic list of the *Instituta Generalis Capituli* then in force. It could easily be memorized. Saint Bernard gave a copy of it to the canons of Prémontré, founded around 1120 by his illustrious friend Norbert of Xanten, who went on to become archbishop of

34. 68 Van Damme, 'Genèse', pp. 55–56.

Magdeburg in 1126. Norbert's successor, abbot Hugh of Fosses, gathered the abbots of his reformed canons regular in chapter around 1128, but this was not yet the authoritative body it would become within a few years in imitation of the chapter of Cîteaux. Hugh had to work out new legislation, and the statutes of Cîteaux seemed the best answer to the needs of his nascent order. In the constitutions of Prémontré there are long passages borrowed almost verbatim from the collection of 'Clairvaux'.

The canons regular of Saint-Victor in Paris and of Arrouaise did somewhat later what the Premonstratensians had done: they borrowed from the Cistercian *Charter*, in the text of the same collection. Other orders or congregations also borrowed from Cîteaux, but, as happened in the case of Chalais, directly from the *Charter of Charity*.[35]

The Book of Usages

The Book of Usages (*Liber Usuum*) is a volume which contains only the daily customs that make up the concrete life of the cistercian monk. The reform of Cîteaux had one objective: the restoration of the Rule of Saint Benedict. But the Rule does not regulate every single personal or community act in monastic life. It leaves unanswered a number of questions about liturgical ceremonies; community exercises in the chapter room, the refectory, dormitory, cloister, workshops, and fields; the particulars of shaving and bleeding; and specific duties of the officers of the monastery—the sacristan, the wardrobe-keeper, and all the rest. The *Charter* of 1119 made obligatory uniformity in every aspect of the monk's life, and this uniformity was based on the concrete life of the abbey of Cîteaux. Yet at Cîteaux the monks followed customs which had been brought from Molesme and adapted to the principle of perfect conformity to the Rule. The abbots who met there each year therefore had to inform themselves on a number of

35. Van Damme, 'Autour', *Collectanea* 20 (1958) 59 n. 55, and 'La Charte de Charité', *Cîteaux* 14 (1963) 81–104.

questions, but they found several collections of usages attributed to the 'monastery' of Cîteaux.[36] The diversity of the texts already recovered shows how difficult, well nigh impossible, it was to attain the desired goal by this approach. It seemed advisable, therefore, to prepare a text for the whole Order. By 1125 Stephen felt that the time had come to write down and collate the practices then in force in his abbey in some systematic way that could be developed and adapted everywhere. This gave rise to the *Officia Ecclesiastica* of Cîteaux. There we find traces of usages inherited from the forebears of the abbey of Molesme, that is, Saint Michel of Tonnerre and Saint Benigne of Dijon.[37] Some two hundred manuscripts, dating from the first centuries of the Order and containing texts either from the twelfth or a later century have been recovered. These texts are often accompanied by other documents or collections of cistercian legislation, such as the *Exordium Parvum*, the *Charter of Charity* in its 1119 or 1165 version; the *Instituta Generalis Capituli*, and the *Usages of the Lay Brothers*, which will be discussed next. Sometimes appended to them were the decisions of the annual chapters called *Statuta Annalia*, which were not contained in the codifications. The title *Book of Usages* is generally given to the codex and refers to the whole collection.

The Usages of the Lay Brothers

Stephen next turned his attention to the lay brothers, who had been admitted on an equal footing with the monks, both spiritually and temporally. He knew, however, that in several monasteries the lay brothers, living on granges far from the abbey, had been neglected by their abbots, especially insofar as their spiritual needs were concerned. He conceived the idea of giving them a rule of

---

36. Zürich, Zentralbibliothek ms Car. C.#175; Tarragona, Bibl. Prov. ms 88; Rome, Biblioteca Nazionale, Fondo Sess., n. 141. The first was edited by Bruno Griesser, '*Die Consuetudines Domus Cisterciensis*', in *Analecta SOC* 3 (1947) 138–146.

37. Bruno Schneider, *Cîteaux und die Benediktinische Tradition* (Roma: Editiones Cistercienses, 1961).

life similar to the usages of the monks, but adapted to their state. This would regulate their life on the granges, their admission, their year of probation and profession, their religious exercises, and their contacts with the abbey.

The introduction of these regulations provides a realistic description of the circumstances which made this little book of *Usages* necessary. From it readers will see the importance Stephen attached to it and the improvements he expected from it:

> Having been entrusted by the bishops with the spiritual care of our lay brothers in the same way as we have that of the monks, I am astonished that some of our abbots give attention to the regular discipline to the monks—as they ought—but show little or no concern for that of the lay brothers. Others hold them in contempt because of their simplicity and think that they need even less food or clothing than do the monks, even though they imperiously assign them to do manual work. Still others, yielding to their complaints, grant more to their bodies than is expedient for their souls, exacting more work from them by treating them more leniently in matters of food and clothing. Both, in one way or another, demand the work but pretend not to see their shortcomings. They studiously impose work which is of little value, while giving them little instruction in what really matters, betraying openly that from the community of lay brothers they are seeking their own gain and not the interests of Jesus Christ. Finally, if the lay brothers, too, have been bought at a great price,[38] why are they, who are patently equals in the grace of redemption, thus discriminated against? Right reason tells us that those who are simple and lacking in education have a greater need of our care and our attention. Therefore, as we have composed the *Usages* of monks out of a need to preserve uniformity in all our actions, so now provision must be made as well for our lay brothers in the following document, which

38. 1 Cor 6:20.

we have decided must be set down to meet the temporal and spiritual needs of the brothers.[39]

Stephen Harding and Cistercian Nuns

Nuns made their first appearance as a feminine branch affiliated with the monks in the Cistercian Order around 1150. This was one of the consequences of the affiliation in 1147 of the small congregation of Obazine, which had an abbey of nuns at Coirux. Its founder, Abbot Stephen of Obazine, continued to be responsible for it.

From its foundation until then, the Cistercian Order had refused to take on the care of monasteries of women. Cistercian abbots were forbidden even to 'bless' nuns, that is, to receive their professions or give them the veil.[40] This prohibition was aimed primarily at abbots who had participated in the foundation of women's houses, for certain abbots on their own initiative had founded monasteries where women, especially those whose husbands had died on crusade or had entered a monastery, could follow their attraction to the religious life. After his return to Molesme, Saint Robert had had under his jurisdiction not only monks but also nuns living in various houses around his abbey. Saint Bernard took an active interest in the monastery of Jully, where his sister Humbelina became prioress in 1128. Walter, the second abbot of Morimond, promoted the establishment of Belfays, an abbey of nuns intended exclusively for women who had been left alone because of the crusades or their husbands' entry into religion. Similarly, Saint Bernard founded Montreuil-sur-Laon, and Hugh of Pontigny organized the monastery of Yerres. As these nuns generally followed observances based on the customs of Cluny, cistercian abbots had to restrict themselves to giving them material aid and moral support, but no regular spiritual direction.[41]

39. According to Trent ms 1711. The text is found in Jacques Lefévre, 'L'evolution des *Usus Conversorum*', in *Collectanea OCR* 21 (1955) 85–86.

40. Van Damme, 'Genèse', p. 42 n. 30, referring to Vincent Hermans, *Commentarius Cisterciensis . . . in Constitutiones ocso* (Rome, 1956) 20.

41. Jean de la Croix Bouton, *Histroire de l'Ordre de Citeaux* (Westmalle: Fiches Cisterciennes, 1959) 117ff.

In the same spirit, Stephen Harding founded the abbey of Tart, called 'cistercian' because its observance was modeled on the observance of Cîteaux. It became an autonomous abbey in the manner of abbeys of monks. This, while not unique, was at least rare at a time when nuns usually lived in priories or sometimes 'double monasteries' in which part of the buildings were occupied by the nuns and another part by monks. Robert of Arbrissel entrusted the governance of his double monasteries to the abbess and not to an abbot. The canons of Prémontré counted a large number of double monasteries in their Order.

The family of the counts of Vergy, generous donors to the abbey of Cîteaux, was the principal benefactor of Tart. Elizabeth, the daughter of Elizabeth of Vergy and Count Savary of Donzy, was its first abbess. Tart evolved into a monastic order with several daughter-houses. After 1150, this order drew increasingly close to the White Monks. Toward the end of the twelfth century, when Prémontré gave up its nuns, many of them transferred to Cîteaux which incorporated them spiritually. Other monasteries of nuns in Belgium and Spain as well as houses founded at the time followed this example. In the course of this evolution, Tart often appealed to its founder, Stephen Harding, to make sure that the Order would continue to support it spiritually and to incorporate it more completely.

Influence Within the Church

A man like Stephen, the originator of great accomplishments and organizer of a renowned Order, had to have attracted the attention of the general public and of highly placed civil and ecclesiastical authorities. But very soon it was Saint Bernard's personality that predominated on all official occasions. The prestige of the father heightened the prestige of the son, and vice versa.

In Paris, a deacon named Stephen discharged the highest offices at the court of Louis VI, 'the Fat'. A letter from the abbot of Clairvaux reminded him of his diaconal responsibilities and reproached him for betraying them by seeking honors and riches. Stephen gave up part of his possessions and retired from public life. A short while later, he became bishop of Paris and led a life worthy of a Church leader. The change displeased the king, whose favor turned to hatred; he had all the possessions of the see of Paris pillaged or destroyed. Deeply humiliated, Stephen went to Cîteaux to seek the help of Stephen Harding, Bernard, and the other leading abbots then assembled in chapter. A letter, unctuous in form but harsh in content, was dispatched to Louis the Fat in the name of Stephen. Although drawn up with the approval of the pope, who had written a similar letter to the king, the chapter's initiative did not produce the desired result. The king simply transferred his pique to another churchman, Archbishop Henry of Sens. He persecuted him on the pretext that he had been installed simonaically. This new victim of the king's anger also had recourse to the cistercian abbots, who exerted all their influence and even invoked Pope Honorius II to bring the conflict to an end. A final letter was sent by the abbot of Clairvaux to the papal chancellor, Haimeric. The affair calmed down slowly and imperceptibly. Henry stayed on in the see of Sens and experienced no further harassment from the king.

The council of Troyes, held in 1128 under the presidency of Cardinal Matthew of Albano, was attended by Abbots Stephen, Bernard, Hugh of Pontigny, and Guy of Trois-Fontaines. Among other disputed matters, it examined the conflict between the king and Bishop Stephen of Paris. Bernard, well-informed about the unfortunate situation in Paris, made himself the spokesman for the cistercian delegation. His help was also solicited by Bishop Henry of Verdun, involved in a dispute with Abbot Fulbert of Cambrai. Bernard acquitted himself successfully. As recompense for his help, he recommended the construction of the cistercian abbey of La Chalade in the diocese of Verdun.[42] On the same occasion Bernard was asked to write a rule for the Knights Templars, who had come from church authorities to Troyes with this request.

42. Angelus Manrique, *Annales Cistercienses* (Lyons: G. Boissat & Laurent, Anisson, 1642) 1:184.

In 1131, a serious disagreement had set the abbey of Saint Stephen in Dijon against that of Saint Seine. The two abbots shared the same name, Herbert. To settle the dispute, Pope Innocent II, well aware of Stephen Harding's legal talents and monastic convictions, named him as mediator. The dispute arose over the churches of Dairé and Estaule. Stephen brought the affair to a satisfactory conclusion and his reputation was hailed in every document on the case.[43]

Valuable Privileges

Cîteaux is often characterized as a wealthy Order whose abbeys are agricultural and industrial centers, without any reference to historical period. We have already had an opportunity to rectify this overly imprecise and summary opinion in discussing the Order's artistic and spiritual accomplishments. But we need also to correct some of the frequently expressed ideas about the real poverty in which the monks were living during the period which concerns us. The large cistercian buildings praised for their architectural purity and solid construction date mostly from the end of the twelfth century. The principles of poverty which governed their life had not yet been abandoned, but the growth of contemporary society, the rise of early capitalism, and great success in their agricultural work, brought in revenues far beyond the monks' expectations. Even so, we can firmly state, without fear of deceiving ourselves about their detachment from worldly goods, that the generations of monks which succeeded those of Saint Robert and Saint Bernard retained, down to 1200, an attitude worthy of their founders. The frequent admonitions of the General Chapter about suppressing every manifestation of luxury are there to prove it.

Morimond was not the only abbey in Stephen Harding's lifetime which narrowly escaped total ruin. Clairvaux suffered periods of great poverty, but Bernard, a man of genius and holiness, had the

43. Anselme Dimier, 'Étienne Harding', *Dictionnaire d'Histoire et Géographie ecclésiastique*, 15: col. 1231.

good fortune to be assisted by priors and cellerars with a talent for administration. Cîteaux was not conspicuous, either for its indigence or its wealth.

A dispute over tithes between the cistercian abbey of Miroir, founded on 5 September 1131 in the diocese of Lyons, and the nearby cluniac priory of Gigny led to the grant of a privilege important for the whole Order. This privilege, granting exemption from tithes, was preceded by another, more restricted, privilege, also connected with the dispute between Le Miroir and Gigny. The authors of the *Histoire Littéraire de la France* tell of the affair in these words:

> This pope Innocent II eager, no doubt, to acknowledge the great services which Saint Bernard had rendered him, freed the monks of Cîteaux from the tithes they had to pay to the monks of Cluny. This privilege aroused complaints and murmurings on the part of the affected parties, but the pope, far from being moved by them, extended it to every other tithe the monks of Cîteaux had to pay. Although the privilege was granted out of consideration for Saint Bernard, we do not see that he was involved in this matter or that he had taken any part in the dispute. Perhaps it was not to his liking or possibly other matters had left him no time for it.[44]

For reasons given at the end of this passage, we believe Bernard had nothing to do with the acquisition of these privileges. The first privilege, whose text is unfortunately lost, was given shortly after Pope Innocent II's visit to Clairvaux, a visit which took place in the summer of 1131. The pontiff was impressed by its discipline, its great poverty and austerity, but most of all by the contrast it made with the abbeys of Saint Denis and Cluny, which he had just visited. The appeal to Rome which the monks of Miroir made at the end of 1131 or in early 1132 was very probably the occasion on

---

44. In a supplementary volume, *Histoire littéraire de Saint Bernard et de Pierre le Venerable* (Paris, 1873) 23.

which the cistercian abbeys were given exemption from the tithes they had to pay cluniac monasteries. A very unusual privilege, indeed, which brought on a spirited reaction at Cluny and led to the spilling of much ink! Peter the Venerable appealed to the pope and to Chancellor Haimeric to obtain the revocation of the privilege which was so damaging to his Order. His two petitions date from November or December 1131, for he expressed his regret that the great monastery of Gigny, stricken with an interdict of forty days for having demanded tithes in violation of the privilege, should be deprived of liturgical functions on Christmas day. He asked that the sanction be suspended at least until he could send a delegation to the pope sometime before Easter to discuss the matter. His pleas did not have the desired effect. On 10 February 1132, while visiting Cluny—where the matter must surely have been thoroughly discussed—the pope confirmed and enlarged the contested privilege by a bull granted to Stephen, abbot of Cîteaux. All that Peter accomplished was the removal of the stigma from his Order through the generalization of the privilege.

Almost certainly, Stephen requested the second privilege. This is not surprising, for he had a greater interest in it than did Bernard. In the first place, he was the immediate superior of the abbey of Miroir, a foundation of Cîteaux. Then, as president of the General Chapter, he was accustomed to requesting and receiving privileges on behalf of the whole Order. Finally, in view of his prestige and merits he, as much as Bernard, had a right to the pope's recognition. Encouraged, no doubt, by some official communication from the pope's entourage, he felt bold enough to ask for the confirmation of certain goods and rights which his abbey or Order already possessed as well as the concession of new favors to his abbey and all other abbeys in the great cistercian family. The contents of the second privilege are:

1. The present and future possessions of the abbey of Cîteaux were confirmed.
2. The abbots of the Order were from then on to be exempted

from attending provincial councils or synods, except when matters of the faith were to be treated in them.

3. The abbey of Cîteaux might choose as its abbot any abbot or monk of the Order. The other abbey might take their abbots from among the monks of the whole Order or, if they made foundations, the abbots of their filiation.

4. The professed lay brothers were no longer under the jurisdiction of the bishop, but under that of their abbots. The duty of almsgiving and hospitality was recalled.

5. All cistercian abbeys were exempted from the payment of tithes.

6. The goods of the Cistercian Order and all its abbots were declared inviolable.[45]

On the seventeenth of the same month, Bernard obtained a similar papal privilege for his abbey. In the intervening seven days the pope continued his journey as far as Lyons, where he signed this bull. By it he acknowledged the merits and rewarded the hard work the abbot of Clairvaux had undertaken for the unity and peace of the Church.[46]

Twilight of a Long Life

Having accomplished all that he had set out to do, Stephen, as old people are wont to do, looked back on his youth and his first steps in the monastic life. He wrote the letter already mentioned to his former confrères at Sherborne, men whom he had left some sixty years earlier. In it he humbly admitted the lack of courage which had caused him to leave the monastery but then praised God for having given him the grace of a new family. His words are like a spiritual testament, a last farewell:

> I, who was alone and poor when I left my country, am now joyfully entering the way of all flesh as a rich and happy man

45. PL 179:122 and Marilier, *Chartes*, n. 90, pp. 92–93.
46. PL 179:126 and Jean Waquet, *Recueil des chartes de l'abbaye de Clairvaux* (Troyes, 1950) n. 4.

surrounded by forty troops, and confidently looking forward to the penny promised to the faithful laborers of the vineyard. So let me exhort Your Charity: strive to increase your good reputation, which has reached even us, by advancing in the virtues, so that moving from what is good to what is better and firmly cleaving to true monastic discipline, you may with body and soul practise charity, chastity, humility and the love of poverty until death and thus be found worthy to see the God of gods. Amen.[47]

The noble thoughts expressed in these lines show that their author had reached the summit of holiness. Although they were addressed to his former confrères at Sherborne, every Cistercian may rightly view them as final advice from a father about to depart this earth.

The allusions to Holy Scripture show how deeply Stephen had familiarized himself with the Word of God. In the most telling reference, he compares himself to Jacob, returning to his native land. Jacob, in times of yore, had left home, taking only a traveler's staff, but he returned a rich man able to set up two camps. Stephen admitted that he had left the cradle of his monastic life without any merit of his own; but now he poured out his heart in praising God, who had blessed his life and given him forty 'camps' or 'troops'[48]— an allusion to the number of abbeys in the Order by this time. About to depart this life and meet God, he appealed to God's mercy to accept the works it had accomplished through him and to count them towards his election.

Old age and illness obliged the saint to give up his abbatial office. It frequently happened in the Middle Ages that a monk, especially a copyist, went blind. This is what happened to Stephen Harding. No longer able to govern his community, he resigned his office for the good of his monks.

47. C. H. Talbot, 'An Unpublished Letter', and Marilier, *Chartes*, n. 88, p. 91.
48. *Turma* in the Vulgate (Genesis 32:10). The *turba* Stephen has, whose meaning could be identical, is perhaps the word he preferred in his recension of the Bible.

This trial was followed by yet another, even more painful. Guy, the abbot of Trois-Fontaines, was elected to succeed him. A monk of Clairvux's filiation, he could not have been elected to Cîteaux without the privilege of 10 February 1132. He was an exceptionally gifted man, a pillar of the Order, a spiritual son and friend of Saint Bernard. The fact that Stephen had requested the privilege leads us to suspect that Guy was his personal candidate to succeed him at Cîteaux. Ordericus Vitalis, writing two or three years after these events, which were apparently well-known in monastic circles, confirmed this interpretation by claiming that 'Guy was elected during Stephen's lifetime and *at his wish*.[49] Stephen's disappointment and grief would have been all the more painful when, shortly after his election, Guy showed himself unworthy of his office:

> On the day of his election, while receiving the customary promise of obedience from the brothers, the great servant of God [Stephen] saw in his soul how the Impure Spirit approached Guy and entered his mouth. Hardly a month passed before the unworthiness of this man became manifest through the Lord's revelation, whereupon the degenerate shoot not planted by the heavenly Father was weeded out of the garden of the elect.[50]

This account from the *Exordium Magnum* is certainly legendary.[51] It may have been invented to hide details which the monks did not want to make public. Guy, outwardly irreproachable, was discovered by Stephen to be guilty of a secret vice which made him into a 'whitened sepulchre'. The exact nature of his vice is not specified anywhere in the contemporary sources and can only be guessed at.

How was Guy deposed? By basing our answer on known historical data and comparing them, we can explain and reconstruct what had happened. Here are the data: first, we know from Manrique

49. Ordericus Vitalis; PL 188:641.
50. (Soligny-la-Trappe, 1884) ch. 24, pp. 98–99.
51. *Exordium Magnum*, ed. B. Griesser (Rome, 1961) 88.

that Guy's deposition was made by a sentence of the General Chapter.[52] Second, the duration of Guy's administration must be estimated at four months.[53] Next, and this is the third element of the solution, his deposition took place at the beginning of 1134 at the latest.[54]

Finally, and this is the last piece of evidence, in 1119 the *Charter of Charity* had prescribed that for the deposition of the abbot of Cîteaux it was necessary to go to the local bishop and his chapter, whereas in 1152 this article of the Charter had been changed and the procedure simplified; recourse to the ordinary is no longer mentioned. The change must, therefore, have been made between 1119 and 1152.

We may reasonably assume that this change was made at the time of Guy's deposition and this—we believe—is how the matter can be explained: Stephen, knowing that the spiritual welfare of his community and of the Order was in danger, and realizing that an immediate solution was necessary, turned to the bishop of Chalon to ask for Guy's deposition in accordance with the *Charter* of 1119. But the bishop and his chapter must have refused to intervene or at least to pronounce the deposition. They may have declined out of principle, to avoid involving themselves in the internal affairs of the Order, or because Guy's case was special in that the offense was a secret one and therefore outside the sanctions of the law. Thus, a decision of the General Chapter became necessary. But because we know that the deposition took place at the beginning of 1134, we must conclude that they did not wait for the regular date of the chapter. Since the *Charter of Charity* had foreseen urgent cases, only the abbots whose monasteries were directly descended from Cîteaux were summoned. This, then, was the chapter which pronounced the sentence of deposition.

The sources are silent and offer no solid hint about Guy's later conduct or about the place where he spent the rest of his life. His

52. Manrique, *Annales*, p. 261.
53. Marilier, *Chartes*, p. 26.
54. *Ibid.*

name does not figure in any of the ancient lists of the abbots of Cîteaux.

Raynald of Bar, a monk of Clairvaux, was elected in his place. His abbot, Bernard, who must surely have promoted his election, was from then on the outstanding figure in the Order. Although the abbot of Clairvaux had previously kept his distance from the governance of the Order out of respect for Stephen, whose talents he acknowledged and whose authority he fully accepted, his prestige and influence very soon eclipsed the personality of his Father Abbot.

This second election and the knowledge that his own son Bernard would be there to watch over Raynald's first steps as abbot and president of the Chapter were like a soothing balm on Stephen's painful wound, inflicted by the scandalous failure of his immediate successor. He succumbed, nevertheless, to the shock of these unfortunate events and on 28 March 1134 returned his soul to God, in the joy of hope and with the abandon of love.

EPILOGUE

ROBERT, ALBERIC AND STEPHEN—three men of God who played different roles, but were wholly united in their drive towards a single goal: a monastic life faithful to its most authentic traditions and, at the same time, one capable of meeting the aspirations of the best of their contemporaries for renewal and regeneration

Their efforts converged in the great monastic movement which, in turn, promoted the general reform of the Church. They contributed from within to the renewal of the Church, which the Divine Spouse wills be forever without spot or wrinkle. Through their personal holiness and the movement they had created, the Founders of Cîteaux purified the Church of imperfections and endowed her with a new spiritual tradition.

Through the centuries, the Church forms a vital link between Eternal God—the source of all holiness and the youthfulness of all life—and the fruit of his almighty power and merciful goodness—humankind on its way towards Paradise.

May the example and intercession of the three Founders help their sons and daughters unremittingly to fulfill their common wish, expressed by Stephen in these words: 'Let them labor on the straight and narrow path [of the Gospel] prescribed by the Rule until death, so that after they have put down the burden of the flesh they may repose happily in rest eternal'. Amen.

SELECT BIBLIOGRAPHY

PRIMARY SOURCES

Auctarium Mortui Maris. Paris: J. P. Migne, 1880. PL 160:391–394.

Domesday Book. Sherborne, Dorset-Chichester: Phillimore, 1983.

Exordium Cistercii. Ed. Tiburtius Hümpfner. Vác: Kapisztrán Nyomda, 1932.

Exordium Magnum Cisterciense. Ed. Bruno Griesser. Rome: Editiones Cistercienses, 1961.

Exordium Parvum. Ed. Joannes-B. Van Damme. *Documenta pro Cisterciensis Ordinis historiae ac juris studio* (q.v.) 5–15.

Guignard, Philippe. *Les Monuments primitifs de la règle cistercienne.* Dijon: Darantière, 1878.

Lanfranc. *Judicium de stabilitate monachi in loco quem posuit.* PL 159:333–336.

Laurent, Jacques, ed. *Cartulaires de Molesme.* 2 vols. Paris: A. Picard & Fils, 1907–1911.

Ljubljana (Laibach) University. *Codex manuscriptus* n. 31.

Manrique, Angelus. *Annales Cistercienses.* Lugduni: G. Boissat & Laurent Anisson, 1641.

Marilier, Jean. *Chartes et documents concernant l'Abbaye de Cîteaux, 1098–1182.* Rome: Editiones Cistercienses, 1961.

Martin, P. *Saint Étienne Harding et les premières récensions de la Vulgate Latine.* Amiens, 1887.

Ordericus Vitalis. *Historia Ecclesiastica.* PL 188:636–642. A critical latin edition with english translation by Marjorie Chibnall is also available: *The Ecclesiastical History of Orderic Vitalis*. Oxford: Clarendon Press, 1969–1980.

Paris. Bibliothèque Saint-Geneviève, *Codex latinus* n. 1207.

Saxonis Gesta Danorum. Compendium, lib. I, in Scriptores Minores Historiae Danicae Medii Aevi, vol. II, 219ff., Ed. Martin C. Gertz. Copenhagen: I Kommission hos G. E. C. Gad, 1917.

Spahr, Kolumban. *Das Leben des hl. Robert von Molesme. Eine Quelle zur Vorgeschichte von Citeaux*. Freiburg in der Schweiz: Paulusdruckerei, 1944.

Talbot, C. Hugh. 'An Unpublished Letter of St Stephen Harding,' *Collectanea Ordinis Cisterciensium Reformatorum* 3 (1936) 68.

Trent (Trento) Biblioteca Communale di Trento, Codex n. 1711.

Türk, Joseph. 'Cistercii Statuta Antiquissima', *Analecta Sacri Ordinis Cisterciensis* 4 (1948) 1- 159.

Van Damme, Joannes-B. *Documenta pro Cisterciensis Ordinis historiae ac juris studio*. Westmalle: Typis Ordinis Cisterciensis, 1959.

Vita beati Petri Juliacensis. PL 185 bis:1257–1270.

William of Malmesbury. *De gestis regum anglorum libri quinque*. PL 179:859–1392, esp. 1286- 1290.

SECONDARY WORKS

Berlière, Ursmer. 'La congrégation Bénédictine de Chalais,' *Revue Bénédictine* 31 (1914–1918).

———. 'Les origines de l'ordre de Cîteaux et l'Ordre Bénédictine au XIIe siècle,' *Revue d'Histoire Ecclésiastique* 1 (1900) 448–471 and 2 (1901) 253–290.

Bouton, Jean de la Croix. *Histoire de l'ordre de Cîteaux*. Westmalle: Fiches Cisterciennes, 1959.

Brito, Bernardo. *Chronica de Cister*. Lisbon, 1602.

Canivez, Joseph-M. 'Le rite cistercien', *Ephemerides Liturgicae* 63 (1949) 276–311.

Cawley, Martin. 'Saint Stephen Harding. A Tribute', *Word and Spirit* 8 (1984) 66–86.

Clémancet, Charles. *Histoire littéraire de S. Bernard, abbé de Clairavux, et de Pierre le Vénérable, abbé de Cluni; qui peut servir de supplement au 12e siècle de L'Histoire litteraire de la France*. Paris: Desaint, 1773.

Dailgairns, J. B. and Herbert Thurston. *Life of St. Stephen Harding Abbot of Cîteaux and Founder of the Cistercian Order*. Westminster, Md.: The Newman Bookshop, 1898, 1942.

Delehaye, Fernand. 'Une Moine: Saint Robert, fondateur de Cîteaux,' *Collectanea OCR* 14 (1952) 83–106.

De Moreaux, Edouard. *Histoire de l'Église de Belgique*. Bruxelles, 1845. Volume III, ch. I: 'Le "martyr" Charle-le-Bon'.

Dereine, Charles. 'La fondation de Cîteaux d'après l'*Exordium Cistercii* et l'*Exordium Parvum*', *Cîteaux* 10 (1959) 125–139.

Dimier, Anselme. 'Étienne Harding,' *Dictionnaire d'histoire et de géographie ecclésiastique*, volume 15: col. 1231.

Ducourneau, Othon. 'De l'institution des Us des convers', Saint Bernard et Son Temps. Dijon: Académie, 1929.

———. *Les origines cisterciennes*. Ligugé: Imprimerie E. Aubin et Fils, 1933.

Folz, Robert. 'Le problème des origines de Cîteaux', *Mélanges Saint Bernard*, Dijon: Académie, 1955. 284–294.

Griesser, Bruno. 'Consuetudines Domus Cisterciensis', *Analecta SOC* 3 (1947) 138–146.

Grill, Leopold. 'Der hl. Bernhard als bisher unerkannter Verfasser des *Exordium Cistercii* und der *Summa Cartae Caritatis*', *Cistercienser-Chronik* 66 (1959) 43–57.

———. 'Morimond, soeur jumelle de Clairvaux', in *Bernard de Clairvaux*. Paris: Alsatia, 1953.

Hallinger, Kassius. 'Woher kommen die Laienbrüder,' *Analecta SOC* 12 (1956) 1–104.

Hoffmann, Eberhard. *Das Konverseninstitut des Cistercienserordens*. Freiburg: Fragnière, 1905.

Hümpfner, Tiburtius. 'Die Bibel des hl. Stephan Harding', *Cistercienser-Chronik* 29 (1917) 73-81.

King, A. A. 'St Stephen Harding and Ireland', *Downside Review* 19 (1941) 305–310.

Knowles, David. 'The Primitive Cistercian Documents', in *Great*

Historical Enterprises. Problems in Monastic History. London: Thomas Nelson, 1963.

Lackner, Bede K. *The Eleventh-Century Background of Citeaux.* Cistercian Studies Series, 8. Cistercian Publications, 1972.

Laurent, Jacques, Ed. *Cartulaires de Molesme.* 2 vols. Paris: A. Picard & Fils, 1907–1911.

————. 'Un fondateur', *Annales de Bourgogne* 12 (1940) 31–36.

Leclercq, Jean. 'L'*Exordium Cistercii* et la *Summa Cartae Caritatis* sont-ils de S. Bernard?', *Revue Bénédictine* 73 (1963) 88–99.

Lefèvre, Jacques. 'L'évolution des *Usus Conversorum*', *Collectanea OCR* 21 (1955) 65.

————. 'Saint Robert de Molesme dans l'opinion monastique du XIIe et du XIIIe siècle', *Analecta Bollandiana* 74 (1956) 50–83.

Lekai, Louis J. *The Cistercians. Ideals and Reality.* Kent, Ohio: Ohio State University Press, 1977.

Lenssen, Seraphim. 'Saint Robert Fondateur de Cîteaux, *Collectanea OCR* 4 (1937) 2–16, 81–96, 161–177.

Luddy, Ailbej. *Centenary Life of St. Stephen Harding.* Dublin: M. H. Gill, 1934.

Marilier, Jean. 'Le vocable *Novum Monasterium* dans les premiers documents cisterciens', *Cistercienser-Chronik* 57 (1950) 81–84.

Masoliver, Alejandro. 'Roberto, Alberico y Esteban Harding: Los Origines de Cister', *Studia Monastica* 26 (1984) 295–297.

Müller, Gregor. *Cîteaux unter dem Abte Alberich.* Bregenz: J. N. Teutsch, 1909.

Oursel, Charles. *Étienne Harding abbé de Cîteaux.* Dijon: Bernigaud et Privat, 1962.

————. 'Les principes et l'esprit des miniatures primitives de Cîteaux', *Cîteaux in de Nederlanden* 6 (1955) 161–172.

Petit, Ernest. *Histoire des ducs de Bourgogne de la race capétienne.* Dijon: Picard, 1885.

Schneider, Bruno. *Cîteaux und die benediktinische Tradition.* Roma: Editiones Cistercienses, 1961.

Spahr, Columbanus. *De fontibus constitutivis primigenii iuris con-*

stitutionalis Sacri Ordinis Cisterciensis. Roma: Thesis Lateran, 1953.

Thierry, Augustin. *Histoire de la Conquête de l'Angleterre par les Normands.* Paris: Just Tessier, 1835.

Trenta, Louis S. *Historians and the Origins of Cîteaux.* Kent: Kent State University (Master's) Thesis, 1969.

Türk, Josip. *'Cisterciensium fratrum Instituta'. Cistercienser-Chronik* 52 (1942) 101–107, 118- 123, 132–141.

Van Damme, Jean-Baptiste. 'Autour des origines cisterciennes', *Collectanea OCR* 20 (1958) 46.

———. 'Genèse des Instituta Generalis Capituli', *Cîteaux* 12 (1961) 43.

———. 'La Charte de Charité de Chalais', *Cîteaux* 14 (1963) 81.

———. 'La constitution cistercienne de 1165', *Analecta SOC* 19 (1964) 51–104.

———. 'Saint Étienne mieux connu', *Cîteaux* 14 (1963) 307–313.

———.'Vir Dei Albericus'. *Analecta SOC* 20 (1964) 153–164.

Warren, H. B. de. 'Le monachisme à l'apparition de Bernard', *Bernard de Clairvaux.* Paris: Alsatia, 1953. 45–63.

Williams, Watkin. 'Saint Robert of Molesme.' *Monastic Studies.* Manchester: Manchester University Press, 1938, 121–131.

———. 'The First Cistercian Era', *Journal of Theological Studies* 32 (1930) 56–61.

CISTERCIAN PUBLICATIONS, INC.
TITLES LISTING

—CISTERCIAN TEXTS—

BERNARD OF CLAIRVAUX

Apologia to Abbot William
Bernard of Clairvaux, Letters of
Five Books on Consideration: Advice to a Pope
Homilies in Praise of the Blessed Virgin Mary
Life and Death of Saint Malachy the Irishman
Love without Measure: Extracts from the
 Writings of St Bernard (Paul Dimier)
On Grace and Free Choice
On Loving God (Analysis by Emero Stiegman)
Parables and Sentences (Michael Casey)
Sermons for the Summer Season
Sermons on Conversion
Sermons on the Song of Songs I-IV
The Steps of Humility and Pride

WILLIAM OF SAINT THIERRY

The Enigma of Faith
Exposition on the Epistle to the Romans
Exposition on the Song of Songs
The Golden Epistle
The Mirror of Faith
The Nature and Dignity of Love
On Contemplating God: Prayer & Meditations

AELRED OF RIEVAULX

Dialogue on the Soul
Liturgical Sermons, I
Mirror of Charity
Spiritual Friendship
Treatises I: On Jesus at the Age of Twelve,
 Rule for a Recluse, The Pastoral Prayer
Walter Daniel: The Life of Aelred of Rievaulx

JOHN OF FORD

Sermons on the Final Verses of the
 Songs of Songs I-VII

GILBERT OF HOYLAND

Sermons on the Songs of Songs I-III
Treatises, Sermons and Epistles

OTHER EARLY
CISTERCIAN WRITERS

Adam of Perseigne, Letters of
Alan of Lille: The Art of Preaching
Amadeus of Lausanne: Homilies in Praise of
 Blessed Mary
Baldwin of Ford: Spiritual Tractates I-II
Gertrud the Great: Spiritual Exercises
Gertrud the Great: The Herald of God's
 Loving-Kindness
Guerric of Igny: Liturgical Sermons I-[II]
Helinand of Froidmont: Verses on Death

Idung of Prüfening: Cistercians and Cluniacs:
 The Case for Cîteaux
Isaac of Stella: Sermons on the Christian Year,
 I-[II]
The Life of Beatrice of Nazareth
Serlo of Wilton & Serlo of Savigny: Seven
 Unpublished Works
Stephen of Lexington: Letters from Ireland
Stephen of Sawley: Treatises

—MONASTIC TEXTS—

EASTERN CHRISTIAN TRADITION

Besa: The Life of Shenoute
Cyril of Scythopolis: Lives of the Monks of
 Palestine
Dorotheos of Gaza: Discourses and Sayings
Evagrius Ponticus: Praktikos and Chapters on
 Prayer
Handmaids of the Lord: Lives of Holy Women
 in Late Antiquity & Early Middle Ages
 (Joan Petersen)
Harlots of the Desert (Benedicta Ward)
John Moschos: The Spiritual Meadow
Lives of the Desert Fathers
Lives of Simeon Stylites (Robert Doran)
Luminous Eye (Sebastian Brock)
Mena of Nikiou: Isaac of Alexandria & St
 Macrobius
Pachomian Koinonia I-III (Armand Veilleux)
Paphnutius: Histories/Monks of Upper Egypt
Sayings of the Desert Fathers
 (Benedicta Ward)
Spiritual Direction in the Early Christian East
 (Irénée Hausherr)
Spiritually Beneficial Tales of Paul, Bishop of
 Monembasia (John Wortley)
Symeon the New Theologian: The Theological
 and Practical Treatises & The Three
 Theological Discourses (Paul McGuckin)
Theodoret of Cyrrhus: A History of the
 Monks of Syria
The Syriac Fathers on Prayer and the Spiritual
 Life (Sebastian Brock)

WESTERN CHRISTIAN
TRADITION

Anselm of Canterbury: Letters I-III
 (Walter Fröhlich)
Bede: Commentary...Acts of the Apostles
Bede: Commentary...Seven Catholic Epistles
Bede: Homilies on the Gospels III
The Celtic Monk (U. Ó Maidín)
Gregory the Great: Forty Gospel Homilies
Life of the Jura Fathers
Maxims of Stephen of Muret

CISTERCIAN PUBLICATIONS, INC.
TITLES LISTING

Meditations of Guigo I, Prior of the
    Charterhouse (A. Gordon Mursall)
Peter of Celle: Selected Works
Letters of Rancé I–II
Rule of the Master
Rule of Saint Augustine
Wound of Love: A Carthusian Miscellany

CHRISTIAN SPIRITUALITY

Cloud of Witnesses: The Development of
    Christian Doctrine (David N. Bell)
Call of Wild Geese (Matthew Kelty)
Cistercian Way (André Louf)
The Contemplative Path
Drinking From the Hidden Fountain
    (Thomas Śpidlík)
Eros and Allegory: Medieval Exegesis of the
    Song of Songs (Denys Turner)
Fathers Talking (Aelred Squire)
Friendship and Community (Brian McGuire)
From Cloister to Classroom
Life of St Mary Magdalene and of Her Sister
    St Martha (David Mycoff)
Many Mansions (David N. Bell)
Mercy in Weakness (André Louf)
Name of Jesus (Irénée Hausherr)
No Moment Too Small (Norvene Vest)
Penthos: The Doctrine of Compunction in the
    Christian East (Irénée Hausherr)
Rancé and the Trappist Legacy
    (A.J. Krailsheimer)
Russian Mystics (Sergius Bolshakoff)
Sermons in a Monastery (Matthew Kelty)
Silent Herald of Unity: The Life of
    Maria Gabrielle Sagheddu (Martha
    Driscoll)
Spirituality of the Christian East
    (Thomas Śpidlík)
Spirituality of the Medieval West
    (André Vauchez)
Tuning In To Grace (André Louf)
Wholly Animals: A Book of Beastly Tales
    (David N. Bell)

—MONASTIC STUDIES—

Community and Abbot in the Rule of
    St Benedict I–II (Adalbert de Vogüé)
Finances of the Cistercian Order in the
    Fourteenth Century (Peter King)
Fountains Abbey and Its Benefactors
    (Joan Wardrop)
The Hermit Monks of Grandmont
    (Carole A. Hutchison)
In the Unity of the Holy Spirit
    (Sighard Kleiner)
Joy of Learning & the Love of God:
    Essays in Honor of Jean Leclercq
Monastic Odyssey (Marie Kervingant)

Monastic Practices (Charles Cummings)
Occupation of Celtic Sites in Ireland
    (Geraldine Carville)
Reading St Benedict (Adalbert de Vogüé)
Rule of St Benedict: A Doctrinal and Spiritual
    Commentary (Adalbert de Vogüé)
Rule of St Benedict (Br. Pinocchio)
St Hugh of Lincoln (David H. Farmer)
Stones Laid Before the Lord (Anselme Dimier)
Venerable Bede (Benedicta Ward)
What Nuns Read (David N. Bell)
With Greater Liberty: A Short History of
    Christian Monasticism & Religious
    Orders (Karl Frank)

—CISTERCIAN STUDIES—

Aelred of Rievaulx: A Study (Aelred Squire)
Athirst for God: Spiritual Desire in Bernard of
    Clairvaux's Sermons on the Song of
    Songs (Michael Casey)
Beatrice of Nazareth in Her Context
    (Roger De Ganck)
Bernard of Clairvaux: Man, Monk, Mystic
    (Michael Casey) [tapes and readings]
Bernardus Magister (Nonacentenary)
Catalogue of Manuscripts in the Obrecht
    Collection of the Institute of Cistercian
    Studies (Anna Kirkwood)
Christ the Way: The Christology of Guerric of
    Igny (John Morson)
Cistercian Abbeys of Britain
Cistercians in Denmark (Brian McGuire)
Cistercians in Medieval Art (James France)
Cistercians in Scandinavia (James France)
A Difficult Saint (Brian McGuire)
Dore Abbey (Shoesmith & Richardson)
A Gathering of Friends: Learning & Spirituality
    in John of Forde (Costello and
    Holdsworth)
Image and Likeness: The Augustinian
    Spirituality of William of St Thierry
    (David Bell)
Index of Authors & Works in Cistercian
    Libraries in Great Britain I (David Bell)
Index of Cistercian Authors and Works in
    Medieval Library Catalogues in Great
    Britian (David Bell)
Mystical Theology of St Bernard
    (Étienne Gilson)
The New Monastery: Texts & Studies on the
    Earliest Cistercians
Nicolas Cotheret's Annals of Cîteaux
    (Louis J. Lekai)
Pater Bernhardus (Franz Posset)
A Second Look at Saint Bernard
    (Jean Leclercq)
The Spiritual Teachings of St Bernard of
    Clairvaux (John R. Sommerfeldt)

CISTERCIAN PUBLICATIONS, INC.
TITLES LISTING

Studies in Medieval Cistercian History (various)
Studiosorum Speculum (Louis J. Lekai)
Three Founders of Cîteaux
    (Jean-Baptiste Van Damme)
Towards Unification with God (Beatrice of
    Nazareth in Her Context, 2)
William, Abbot of St Thierry
Women and St Bernard of Clairvaux
    (Jean Leclercq)

MEDIEVAL RELIGIOUS
—WOMEN—

Lillian Thomas Shank and John A. Nichols, editors
Distant Echoes
Hidden Springs: Cistercian Monastic Women
    (2 volumes)
Peace Weavers

—CARTHUSIAN—
TRADITION

Call of Silent Love (A Carthusian)
Freedom of Obedience (A Carthusian)
Guigo II: The Ladder of Monks & Twelve
    Meditations (Colledge & Walsh)
Interior Prayer (A Carthusian)
Meditations of Guigo II (A. Gordon Mursall)
Prayer of Love and Silence (A Carthusian)
Way of Silent Love (A Carthusian Miscellany)
Wound of Love (A Carthusian Miscellany)
They Speak by Silences (A Carthusian)
Where Silence is Praise (A Carthusian)

-STUDIES IN CISTERCIAN-
ART & ARCHITECTURE

Meredith Parsons Lillich, editor
Volumes II-V are now available

—THOMAS MERTON—

Climate of Monastic Prayer (T. Merton)
Legacy of Thomas Merton (P. Hart)
Message of Thomas Merton (P. Hart)
Monastic Journey of Thomas Merton (P. Hart)
Thomas Merton/Monk (P. Hart)
Thomas Merton on St Bernard
Toward an Integrated Humanity
    (M. Basil Pennington, ed.)

CISTERCIAN LITURGICAL
—DOCUMENTS SERIES—

Chrysogonus Waddell, ocso, editor
Hymn Collection of the...Paraclete
Institutiones nostrae: The Paraclete Statutes
Molesme Summer-Season Breviary (4 volumes)
Old French Ordinary & Breviary of the Abbey
    of the Paraclete (2 volumes)

Twelfth-century Cistercian Hymnal
    (2 volumes)
The Twelfth-century Cistercian Psalter
Two Early Cistercian *Libelli Missarum*

-STUDIA PATRISTICA XVIII-
Volumes 1, 2 and 3

❖ ❖ ❖ ❖ ❖ ❖ ❖ ❖ ❖ ❖ ❖ ❖

Editorial queries & advance book
information should be directed to the
Editorial Offices:

Cistercian Publications
1201 Oliver Street
Western Michigan University
Kalamazoo, Michigan 49008
Tel: (616) 387-8920 • Fax: (616) 387-8921

• • •

Customers may order
these books through booksellers
or directly by contacting the warehouse
at the address below:

Cistercian Publications
Saint Joseph's Abbey
167 North Spencer Road
Spencer, Massachusetts 01562-1233
Tel: (508) 885-8730 • Fax: (508) 885-4687
email: cistpub@spencerabbey.org

• • •

Canadian Orders:
Novalis
49 Front Street East, Second Floor
Toronto, Ontario M5E 1B3
Telephone: 416-363-3303 1-800-387-7164
Fax: 416-363-9409

• • •

British & European Orders:
Cistercian Publications
Mount Saint Bernard Abbey
Coalville, Leicester LE67 5UL
Fax: [44] (1530) 81.46.08

• • •

Cistercian Publications is a non-profit
corporation. Its publishing program is
restricted to monastic texts in translation
and books on the monastic tradition.

A complete catalogue of texts in
translation and studies on early,
medieval, and modern monasticism is
available, free of charge, by contacting
any of the addresses above.